Democracy and the Public Service

PUBLIC ADMINISTRATION AND DEMOCRACY

SERIES EDITOR   ROSCOE C. MARTIN

FORTHCOMING
EMMETTE S. REDFORD
Democracy in the Administrative State

OTHER VOLUMES ARE IN PREPARATION

Democracy and the Public Service

FREDERICK C. MOSHER

Professor of Political Science
The University of California at Berkeley

New York
Oxford University Press
London Toronto

To the memory of my father

WILLIAM E. MOSHER

who devoted much of his

thought and his life work

to

democracy and the public service

Prefatory Note

Some of the material on professional education and the professions in the public service, particularly in Chapters 2 and 4 which follow, grew out of research conducted in 1966 and 1967 with the support of the Center for Research and Development in Higher Education, the University of California at Berkeley.

I am indebted to Mr. Keith Axtell for his effective investigations during 1966 on employment practices of governmental agencies in their quests for professional personnel.

Finally, I should like to express my appreciation to Dean Stephen K. Bailey, Professor Roscoe C. Martin, and others at Syracuse University who encouraged this volume through their invitation to lecture at Syracuse in the summer of 1966; and to other faculty and student colleagues at both Berkeley and Syracuse for their sympathetic and critical hearing and reading of these remarks. I have taken advantage of more of their comments than I could possibly acknowledge.

Berkeley, Fall 1967   F.C.M.

Foreword

For the last several years the Maxwell Graduate School of Syracuse University has offered a graduate course titled Public Administration and Democracy. The course has occupied a prominent place in the school's curriculum from its inception, and more recently it has been made a requirement for those engaged in the professional study of administration. Its central purposes are to explore the relations between democracy and administration, to examine the seeming conflicts between the two, and in the end to reconcile the requirements of the administrative state with those of the democratic state.

From its beginning distinguished visitors have lectured in the course, and for the last few years visiting professors have shared equally in its conduct. From this sharing has evolved a plan to publish an annual volume based on the lectures delivered in the course by the guests. Each professor approaches the general subject from his own vantage point, contributing lectures harmonious with his personal experiences and observations and reflecting his own point of view. The general title of the series of books will be that of the course which provides the forum. Each volume will of course carry its own title, one appropriate to the subject with which it deals.

This is the first volume in the new series, Public Administration and Democracy. In it Professor Mosher has chosen to treat of democracy and the public service. His emphasis is on trends and issues in the American public service of today—

philosophical and ideological background, the various systems of public employment and the relations among them, the public service and the educational system, and the expanding roles of the professions and of collective organizations in the public service—always with an eye to their significance for the traditions, the institutions, and the practice of democracy in America.

Those concerned with public affairs are already in Professor Mosher's debt because of his growing list of probing, thoughtful publications. We at Syracuse University are pleased both to acknowledge that debt and to add measurably to it through sponsorship of this book.

ROSCOE C. MARTIN

Contents

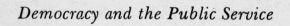

Democracy and the Public Service

1

The Issues

THIS BOOK UNDERTAKES no very exquisite or precise definition of democracy. Nor does it aspire to comprehend all the
facets of democracy: majorities and their powers; minorities
and their protections; nominations and elections; political
representation; the immunities of citizens; or even administration, viewed as a powerful and anonymous entity in its relations with individual citizens. My focus in this volume is
upon the public service itself, and particularly upon the appointive public service, in its relation to democracy both as
an idea and as a way of governance. For this purpose it seems
unnecessary to dwell upon disputable definitions of polyarchy
or consensual elite or similiar intellectual constructs. My
premises are relatively clear and limited: that

1. governmental decisions and behavior have tremendous influence upon the nature and development of our society,
   our economy, and our policy;
2. the great bulk of decisions and actions taken by governments
   are determined or heavily influenced by administrative
   officials, most of whom are appointed, not elected;
3. the kinds of decisions and actions these officials take depend
   upon their capabilities, their orientations, and their
   values; and
4. these attributes depend heavily upon their backgrounds, their
   training and education, and their current associations.

1

Only recently have we had many studies about public executives—about who they are, where they came from, what kinds of preparation and experience they bring to their jobs; and what kinds of objectives they pursue. Many political scientists prefer to deal with the concepts and ideas of old thinkers, of whom few were concerned with administration; or with items they can count—citizen votes, legislative votes, or attitudes as measured through surveys. They have given rather little attention to administration and administrators as a significant element in government.

Perhaps the most concise, simplest, most widely accepted definitions of democracy were those implicit in the Gettysburg Address of Abraham Lincoln. Our nation was one "conceived in liberty and dedicated to the proposition that all men are created equal." And our Civil War was to ensure the survival of government "of the people, by the people, for the people." Clearly the one phrase of the triad which is distinctive for democracy is the second one, "by the people." The first would apply to government of any stripe, and the third to any of paternalistic flavor. But what does "by the people" mean? By *all* the people? If not, by which people? The early, hopeful answer was the former—*all the people,* deciding matters through discussion and debate and vote as exemplified by the Greek city-state and the New England town meeting.[1] Even this elementary pattern could not by itself be fully effective in the community because meetings could not be assembled on the hour every day to handle the continuing problems of government. So was devised the method, once removed from the people, of governance by individuals elected by the people, answerable to them and removable by them— i.e. representatives. Preferably, such officers would serve short terms within narrowly circumscribed zones of discretion and would be forbidden to serve more than one or two terms in office. Although we commonly associate the

1. Though in neither case was participation open to anywhere near *all* the people.

elected representative officer with legislatures and chief executives, the basic concept has applied widely in this country to administrative and judicial officers as well.

Reliance upon popularly elected representatives is one step removed from direct participative democracy. A second step occurs when officers so chosen select and delegate powers to other officers, appointed and removable by them. As the dimensions of the administrative tasks of government grew these came greatly to outnumber the elective officers; and for a period in U.S. history, a substantial part of the public service were politically appointive and removable officers and employees. A third step away from direct democracy is taken with the designation of personnel who are neither elected nor politically appointive and removable, but rather are chosen on bases of stated criteria—social class or caste, family, general competence, specialization in given tasks and skills, etc. —and, once appointed, are protected from removal on political grounds. It is now of course clear that in every developed country in the world the vast majority of public officers and employees are in this category; that many of them command specialized knowledges and skills which give them unique competence in some subject-matter fields—competence that neither the people nor their elected or appointed political officers possess. It is also obvious that they influence —or make—decisions of great significance for the people, though within an environment of constraints, controls, and pressures which itself varies widely from one jurisdiction to another, from one field or subject to another, and from one time to another.

The accretion of specialization and of technological and social complexity seems to be an irreversible trend, one that leads to increasing dependence upon the protected, appointive public service, thrice removed from direct democracy. Herein lies the central and underlying problem to which this volume is addressed: how can a public service so constituted be made to operate in a manner compatible with democracy?

How can we be assured that a highly differentiated body of public employees will act in the interests of all the people, will be an instrument of all the people? My focus in the pages that follow is upon the appointive administrative services, those sectors that are twice and thrice removed from direct democracy. My primary concern is with our experience, our practices, and our directions in the United States; but I include some references to other countries for purposes of contrast and comparison.

In the paragraphs that follow in this chapter, I should like to state some of the principal themes and sub-issues which have underlain the basic problem as it has evolved in American thinking. My purpose is to define and to establish a terminology. All the topics suggested here are treated later on in various connections. They include: policy-politics and administration; responsibility; representation and representativeness; mobility; participation; elitism; the rights of public servants.

POLICY-POLITICS AND ADMINISTRATION

The concept that policy should be determined by politically responsible officials, institutionally separated from the execution of policy—i.e. administration—and the arguments attendant upon it are relatively recent in political and intellectual history. One finds little reference to them in the writings of the great political thinkers, and this perhaps reflects the general lack of concern about administration anyway. In much of this writing, there seems to have been an implicit assumption that administration is the obedient and willing pawn of whoever controls it; the primary issue then is the locus of control. The separation of policy from administration has been equated with the separation of the legislative from the executive power, but the identification in both theory and practice has been a very rough one. In our own Constitutional debates and early political history, it was hardly contemplated that the executive would be or should be powerless on matters of national policy, and in fact certain specific powers with respect to policy were granted him in the Constitution itself. The emergence of the doctrine of institutional dichotomy between policy and administration seems both logically and historically to have followed two basic developments. First was the rise of representative democracy in the Western countries during the eighteenth and nineteenth centuries, expressed primarily through legislative bodies and the emergence of political parties. One of the chief objects of contest became the control of administration —of its positions, its powers, and its policy influence. Second was the recognition of the need for a permanent, protected, and specialized civil service. This recognition arose in some places (as in the United States) primarily from moral indignation at the corruption and excesses of political patronage, and in others primarily from the obvious necessity for adequate skills, knowledge, and experience within administration. How does one square a permanent civil service—which neither the people by their vote nor their representatives by their appointments can replace—with the principle of government "by the people"?

The responses to the problem took somewhat different forms and emphases in different countries, though all were essentially compatible. On the Continent and stemming principally from Germany and Austria, the principal emphasis was upon law—natural law and civil law. Administration is essentially the business of carrying out the affairs of state in accordance with law and due process. The laws expressing public policies are made by the people's representatives in Parliament. In Britain, the Parliament, consisting again of elected representatives of the people, is supreme; the cabinet is a committee of Parliament, removable by the latter. The permanent civil service consists of neutral, impartial individuals who can and will serve any cabinet with equal loyalty and devotion. In the United States, we have taken something from both camps. Our government too is conceived as one of laws rather than of men, and lawyers have long been the largest single occupational group in the top echelons of the public service. Our permanent, protected civil service, which, interestingly, does not yet include lawyers, would be impartial and neutral like its British counterpart. It would carry out policies determined elsewhere, either by the people directly (through initiative and referendum) or by their elected representatives in legislative bodies. In short, there would be a clean division between those responsible for determining policy (the people and their elected representatives) and those responsible for carrying it out (the appointive public service).

The developments in recent decades in the "real world" of government have brought to the policy-administration dichotomy strains which have grown almost beyond the point of toleration.[2] In fact, on the theoretical plane, the finding of a viable substitute may well be the number one problem of public administration today. But this concept, like most others, dies hard. There are built-in obstacles of motivation in favor of perpetuating it. By and large, legislators prefer not to derogate their importance by advertising that it is smaller than it appears to be, and when they do it is usually to denounce administrative (or judicial) "usurpation" of legislative power. Likewise, administrators—especially those in specialized professions—prefer not to advertise, or even to recognize, that they are significantly influencing policy for fear of provoking such charges. Finally, many students of government—as I have already suggested—prefer to study those subjects which are amenable to scientific, objective, and quantifiable treatment. A declaration that these topics are somewhat less important than they seem would be self-defeating. For all three groups—elected officers, appointed administrators, and political scientists—the policy-adminis-

2. These developments are discussed in subsequent chapters, especially 3 and 4.

tration dichotomy is a convenient crutch—or myth—to support and justify their current interests.

RESPONSIBILITY

Responsibility may well be the most important word in all the vocabulary of administration, pubic and private. But it has a confusing wealth of different meanings and shades of meanings, of which I here identify two. The first, *objective responsibility,* connotes the responsibility of a person or an organization *to* someone else, outside of self, *for* some thing or some kind of performance. It is closely akin to *accountability* or *answerability.* If one fails to carry out legitimate directives, he is judged *irresponsible,* and may be subjected to penalties. In a broad sense, the dichotomy between policy and administration depends upon objective responsibility; it assumes that the administrator will carry out policy determinations decided upon elsewhere, whether or not he likes or approves of them. Responsibility is also essential to predictability; if a person does not behave responsibly, his behavior cannot be predicted.

In the classical approach to organization, responsibility is the first essential of hierarchy. Viewing organization from the top down, as most classicists have, we may describe the organizational process in four steps:

1. the definition and delegation of duties (read responsibilities) to a subordinate
2. the provision to said subordinate of resources (in terms of money, people, facilities, and powers) necessary to carry out his responsibilities
3. the measurement and evaluation of accomplishments by the subordinate against his assigned responsibilities
4. the imposition of sanctions for failure to carry out responsibilities or rewards for performance beyond the "call of duty" (read responsibility)

Precedent to the steps listed above is the determination of purposes, which according to the classicists should be dictated by legislative bodies. It should be noted too that authority in this system is a derivative of responsibility, not the reverse (Step 2). Authority should be provided from above to match responsibility—no more, no less. A great many— probably most—of the principles urged by organizational reform groups in recent decades stemmed from, or at least were consistent with, this view of responsibility in the organizational process. They include:

clear delineation of responsibilities
responsibility to one, and only one, superior (unity of command)
delegation of authority and means for carrying out responsibilities
improved measurement of performance (including inspection)
rewards and sanctions appropriate to performance

A quite different connotation attaches to the second meaning of responsibility, which is *subjective* or *psychological*. Its focus is not upon to whom and for what one *is* responsible (according to the law and the organization chart) but to whom and for what one *feels* responsible and *behaves* responsibly. This meaning is more nearly synonymous with identification, loyalty, and conscience than it is with accountability and answerability. And it hinges more heavily upon background, the processes of socialization, and current associations in and outside the organization than does objective responsibility. It introduces the possibility—indeed the inevitability—of competition and conflict among responsibilities. This was pointed out long ago by Chester Barnard,[3] who observed that the higher an executive rose in the hierarchy the more complex were the competing senses of responsibility to which he was subject. Later Arthur Maass endeavored to identify and evaluate competing objects of responsibility of administrative agencies on the basis of cer-

3. In *The Functions of the Executive* (Cambridge, Harvard University Press; 1938), especially Chapter XVII.

tain normative criteria.[4] He mentions responsibilities to:

the people at large (which, as a general proposition, he disap-
    proves)
the people in pressure groups (which for certain limited pur-
    poses he approves)
the legislature (which he feels should only be indirect through
    the chief executive)
the chief executive (which he feels should be direct)
profession (for development and application of professional
    standards)
the courts (which he does not discuss).

Curiously, for a study dedicated primarily to a highly cohesive, unified body of personnel, the Corps of Engineers, Maass
does not mention responsibility to the *Corps* itself, a matter
which would seem of considerable importance in understanding and evaluating the behavior of its personnel.

Subjective responsibility, if one concedes its legitimacy as
an element in government at all, raises immediate and obvious questions about the strength and reliability of objective
responsibility. If one feels responsible in one direction, which
is counter to the directives he receives from above, and modi-
fies his behavior accordingly, what reliance may be placed
upon his objective responsibility to his superior? A similar
question may be framed to attack the underpinning of the alleged dichotomy between policy and administration. If an
individual *feels* responsible in directions other than to his
boss, or if the top boss feels responsible in directions other
than carrying out legislative mandates, what assurance do we
have that policy will in fact be carried out in accordance with
the intention of the representatives of the people? One version of the issue between objective and subjective responsibil-

4. In "Introduction: Gauging Administrative Responsibility," *Muddy
Waters: The Army Engineers and the Nation's Rivers* (Cambridge, Harvard
University Press, 1951). This essay first appeared in *Public Administration Re-
view* in 1949 under joint authorship with Lawrence J. Radway.

ity was argued many years ago in an interchange of articles by Herman Finer and C. J. Friedrich.[5] Finer placed his entire faith on objective responsibility, which he identified with democracy. "Democratic systems are chiefly embodiments of the first mentioned notion of responsibility ('objective') , and dictatorial systems chiefly of the second ('subjective')." [6] Friedrich found this view quite unrealistic, declaring that: ". . . the responsible administrator is one who is responsive to these two dominant factors: technical knowledge and popular sentiment." [7] He urged the necessity of professional responsibility, enforceable principally by fellow professionals and by one's own conscience. As I suggest later, in Chapter 4, the developments since World War II appear to give support to Friedrich's view. Our dependence upon professionals is now so great that the orientations, value systems, and ethics which they bring to their work and which they enforce on one another are a matter of prime concern to those who would strengthen the democratic system.

REPRESENTATION AND REPRESENTATIVENESS

Loosely associated with the idea of subjective responsibility is that of representativeness of the people in the appointive public service. The general idea is an old one in this country. Certainly it was implicit and sometimes explicit in the Jacksonian spoils system; in the continuing opposition to a bureaucratic class; in the provision of the Pendleton Act for proportionate representation of the different states in appointments in Washington; in the long-established general practice of staffing most field offices with local residents. It is also reflected in the way in which the national administration

5. Friedrich's article originally appeared in *Public Policy: A Yearbook of the Graduate School of Public Administration, 1940.* Finer's reply was published in *Public Administration Review,* 1 (Summer 1941). The quotations used here were taken from Donald C. Rowat (ed.), *Basic Issues in Public Administration* (New York, The Macmillan Company, 1961).
6. Rowat, op. cit. p. 468.
7. Ibid. p. 462.

has been structured. Most but not all interest groups and occupational clusters have some organizational expression in the departments, agencies, bureaus, and divisions of the national government, the leadership of which is expected to be responsive to the group to a greater or lesser extent. In fact, the demand of groups for representation in the structure is itself implicit acknowledgment that administration is involved in policy matters. Thus, for example, we have:

a Department of Agriculture for farmers
a Department of Labor for the working man (and a Women's Division for working women)
a Department of Commerce for business (and a Small Business Administration for small business men)
a Children's Bureau for children (or more accurately for groups interested in child welfare)
a Veterans Administration for veterans
a National Science Foundation for scientists
a Bureau of Fish and Wildlife for sportsmen
an Office of Education for educators

and so on, almost *ad infinitum*. A current expression of the demand for representation in the national administration is the insistence of some groups that the poverty program be governed and staffed in large part by the poor.

In spite of these rather clear manifestations of the idea of representativeness in the public service, there has been rather little articulation of a theory of "representative bureaucracy" until quite recently. Some writers have, in the last thirty years, endeavored to promote such a concept as an antidote or a supplement to legislative inadequacies and as a substitute for the shaky dichotomy of policy-politics and administration (see Chapter 3). And it may well be that, ere too long, some of the avowed political theorists will find room to discuss it in their larger discourses on political philosophy.

But there is a confusion of at least two quite different meanings of representativeness, as there is confusion in the meanings of responsibility. First, there is an *active* (or responsible) *representativeness* wherein an individual (or administrator) is expected to press for the interests and desires of those whom he is presumed to represent, whether they be the whole people or some segment of the people. Some hold that, like objective responsibility, assurance of continuing active representativeness requires some degree of answerability for decisions made and actions taken to those who are being represented. And answerability implies the possibilities of rewards for jobs well done and sanctions for failures. For the career public servant, of course, the ultimate sanction of political representatives—removal from office—is seldom available. But other and more subtle rewards and sanctions are possible: unfavorable publicity, reassignment, reduction of responsibilities, withholding of promotion, etc.

It may be noted that active representativeness run rampant within a bureaucracy would constitute a major threat to orderly democratic government. The summing up of the multitude of special interests seeking effective representation does not constitute the general interest. The strengths of different private interest groups within administration are vastly unequal, and the establishment of anything approaching equity would be nearly impossible. And the dangers of interest representation are reflected—perhaps excessively—in the conflict of interest laws. Thus there are very real problems in the development of a rounded concept of representative bureaucracy within our democratic framework.

The *passive* (or sociological) meaning of representativeness concerns the source of origin of individuals and the degree to which, collectively, they mirror the total society. It may be statistically measured in terms, for example, of locality of origin and its nature (rural, urban, suburban, etc.), previous occupation, father's occupation, education, family income, family social class, race, religion. A public service, and more specifically the leadership personnel of a public service, which is broadly representative of all categories of the population in these respects, may be thought of as satisfying Lincoln's prescription of government "by the people" in a limited sense. At least, such a breadth of characteristics and origins suggests the absence of any single ruling class from which public personnel are drawn or of any single perspective and set of motivations. But this does not necessarily mean that a public servant with given background and social characteristics will *ipso facto* represent the interests of others with like backgrounds and characteristics in his behavior and decisions. A man born and brought up in Ohio who takes a job in Washington is not bound to represent the interests of Ohioans; in fact vigorous disciplinary measures may be invoked to prevent such partiality. The same might be said of a farmer's son or a farmer representing the interests of farmers; or of a business man, or a college graduate, or a poor man.

I lay stress on the distinction between active and passive representativeness because it seems to me there has been a good deal of confusion on the matter in the recent literature about public executives. The fact is that we know too little about the relationship between a man's background and pre-employment socialization on the one hand, and his orientation and behavior in office on the other. Undoubtedly, there are a good many other intervening variables: the length of time in the organization, or the time-distance from his background; the nature and strength of the socialization process within the organization; the nature of the position (in some, particularly among political appointees, incumbents are expected to represent actively; in others, active representation may be expressly forbidden and incumbents encouraged to "lean over backwards" to avoid the appearance of partiality) ; the length and content of preparatory education; the strength of associations beyond the job and beyond the agency; etc.

While passive representativeness is no guarantor of democratic decision-making, it carries some independent and symbolic values that are significant for a democratic society. A broadly representative public service, especially at the level of leadership, suggests an *open service* in which access is available to most prople, whatever their station in life, and in which there is *equality of opportunity*. These are values which Americans have honored—in speech if not always in deed—for more than a century. They were significant aspirations in the development of both the spoils system and the civil service system. The importance of passive representativeness often resides less in the behaviors of public employees than in the fact that the employees who are there are there at all. Negatively, its significance rests on the absence, or conspicuous underrepresentation, of certain categories of people, suggesting or reflecting barriers to their entry or advancement. Severest among the violations of passive representativeness in this country today are the shortages of minority races in middle and upper levels of service in most public (as well as private) agencies.

MOBILITY

A high degree of passive representativeness among the leadership personnel in government may then be construed as one index of a relatively mobile society; and if the degree of mobility in government is relatively higher than in other leadership positions in society, public employment may be considered a principal channel of, and contributor to, social mobility. There is a good deal of evidence that a high degree of mobility—accompanied as it is with concepts of equality of opportunity and an open and free society—is both widely valued in the United States and equated with democracy itself. In spite of ideologies to the contrary, Lipset and Bendix did not find social mobility, as they defined it, to be significantly higher in the United States than in many countries of western Europe, though in all it was relatively high in comparison with non-industrial societies.[8] The studies by W. Lloyd Warner and others of business and federal executives in

8. Seymour Martin Lipset and Reinhard Bendix, *Social Mobility in Industrial Society* (Berkeley, University of California Press, 1959), especially Chapters II and III.

the United States suggest that governmental leadership reflects a somewhat higher degree of mobility than does business, and that for both it is probably increasing.[9]

But there are several kinds and definitions of mobility. Sociologists, committed as many of them are to the search for vertical differentiations between classes and statuses, tend to define it in terms of shifts from one level to another. "The term 'social mobility' refers to the process by which individuals move from one position to another in society—positions which by general consent have been given specific hierarchical values." [10] The commonest, though admittedly an imperfect, index of rank in the social pecking order is occupation, ranging on the lower end from manual labor (including farming) up through skilled labor to white collar, professional, and elite. It may be noted that a relatively high rate of upward mobility on such a scale is an inevitable accompaniment to a developing industrial society—whether it be cause or effect. As farming becomes more mechanized and more efficient, farm population declines relatively, perhaps absolutely. Mechanization and, later, automation limit the growth of manual workers in industry. Meanwhile, organizations grow, trade grows, professional services grow, management grows.

There are, however, other kinds of mobility whose importance may soon surpass upward social mobility in the economic and political world. In an increasingly specialized society—and a developing society is almost by definition an increasingly specialized one—it becomes more difficult (and more academic) to draw horizontal lines across many specialties and define vertical classes. Each specialty is likely to develop its own internal pecking order. Upward mobility within a given specialty field may be very substantial and rapid if the demands for the services of that field are growing; of course, the reverse is equally true. As the educational requisites for

9. Particularly W. Lloyd Warner, Paul P. Van Riper, Norman H. Martin, and Orvis F. Collins, *The American Federal Executive* (New Haven, Yale University Press, 1963).

10. Lipset and Bendix, op. cit. pp. 1–2.

entering a particular specialized field develop, and as career patterns within the field harden, mobility *across* specialties becomes increasingly inhibited. In other words, increasing, and increasingly specialized, education, vocationally oriented, has the double effect of facilitating upward mobility within particular fields of endeavor and discouraging interoccupational mobility. It may be noted in this connection that whether or not a given type of specialization has higher social standing than another may be quite irrelevant.

I may mention two other kinds of mobility, both of some importance in the governmental world. One is mobility as between different employers: public and private; federal and state and city and county—and international agency; one type of agency and another at the same level; and even among different sections and units in the same agency. The restraints against such movements have recently been the source of a good deal of concern in governmental circles and were the object of a major conference (of the American Assembly) in 1966. It may be noted that mobility in all of these regards may have a considerable impact upon representativeness, both active and passive. Another style of mobility is geographic, historically very high in the United States but today, in some parts of the country and among some groups of people, very low indeed.

In this connection, Warren G. Bennis recently predicted a very greatly increased job mobility in the future in which shifts from job to job, from employer to employer, and from place to place would become common.[11] This may well come about; but unless massive efforts are made toward retraining in middle age, it is at least doubtful that such a trend would extend to changes from specialty to specialty.

Finally, there is another common type of distinction in treatments of mobility: that between intergenerational mobility, measured by the difference between the vocation and

<hr>

11. In *Changing Organizations: Essays on the Development and Evolution of Human Organization* (New York, McGraw-Hill Book Company, 1966), p. 11.

status of son or daughter and parents, and intragenerational mobility, that occurring during the educational and working career of a given person. The available data indicate that intergenerational mobility to executive positions in America has been relatively high—as one would expect—over the present and past two generations; and it has been somewhat higher for federal than for business executives.[12] But with the increasing preponderance of technically and professionally trained executives (discussed in Chapter 4), it is probable that intragenerational mobility across occupational lines is on the decline.

PARTICIPATION

Over the past three decades, there has been a substantial movement in the direction of bringing into the managerial processes and decisions of large organizations the ideals and techniques of democracy through greater participation by the officers and employees themselves in the reaching of organizational decisions. Such a system, juxtaposed against the traditional orthodoxy of authoritarian decision-making from the top down, has been advocated by a growing number of students, consultants, and practitioners in organizations, particularly in the world of private business.[13] The arguments for more participative management are many and diverse:

better decisions because more knowledge and opinions would be brought to bear
better morale and less resistance to change
greater degree of *self-actualization* on the part of employees, who under an authoritarian system of formal organization are treated as children and inferiors
greater organizational *effectiveness and efficiency*

12. Warner, *et al., op. cit.*
13. For a more extensive treatment of this subject as it applies to government organizations, see the cases and the analytical comment in Frederick C. Mosher (ed.), *Governmental Reorganizations: A Case Book* (New York, The Bobbs-Merrill Company, 1967).

greater degree of *commitment* to organization and larger stake
    in its decisions and actions on part of employees who
    have actively contributed to determining its destinies
development within organizations of the principles and ideals un-
    derlying democracy: respect for the dignity of the indi-
    vidual, egalitariansim, protection of minorities—and
    majorities—from arbitrary action
employee development

The mechanics of participative democracy within an organization may include any or all of the following: collegial rather
than authoritarian devices in reaching decisions; relaxing of
vertical lines of authority and responsibility in formal structures; increased decentralization and delegation; permissive
supervision; T-Groups for encouragement of frank individual
expression of opinions and attitudes; administration "by
objective" rather than "by means" and controls; in the extreme, actual voting on basic issues. There is neither space nor
need to discuss and evaluate these types of measures here; nor
need we appraise the desirability and feasibility of participative administration in organizations in general. As will be
discussed later (in Chapters 4 and 5), there has already developed a great deal of collegial decision-making in many public
agencies, particularly those which are largely controlled by
single professional groups. But I would point out that *democracy within administration,* if carried to the full, raises a
logical dilemma in its relation to *political democracy.* All
public organizations are presumed to have been established
and to operate for public purposes—i.e. purposes of the people. They are authorized, legitimized, empowered, and usually supported by authorities outside of themselves for broad
purposes initially determined outside of themselves. To what
extent, then, should "insiders," the officers and employees, be
enabled to modify their purposes, their organizational arrangements, and their means of support? It is entirely possible
that internal administrative democracy might run counter to
the principles and objectives of political democracy in which

the organizations of government are viewed as instruments of
public purpose.

ELITISM

I hesitate to introduce the word *elite* in this discussion of
the American public service because it has so many varying
definitions and connotations even among the more rigorous
social scientists. Furthermore, like such words as bureaucrat
and establishment, its sense is often pejorative, even evil—
very nearly synonymous with ruling class, dictatorship, or
aristocracy. Yet, elites have occupied the attention of a great
many political and social philosophers from the time of Aris-
totle through Pareto, Mosca, Saint-Simon, and Mannheim to
Lasswell and C. Wright Mills—to mention only a few. At the
present time, one can hardly read anything in the field of comparative administration without almost tiresome repetition of
the word "elite," particularly as it is applied to societies
somewhere along the road from traditional to modern. This
may be one of the sources of our difficulties with the term:
that it is a simple, useful, and perhaps essential concept for
the understanding of relatively simple, usually undemocratic,
social and political systems as in the medieval and early
national states of the West and currently in a good part of the
non-Western world. But application of the term to a developed, highly specialized, and differentiated society invites
oversimplification.

The central idea of the elite (or equivalent expressions) is
that a small group in a given society is differentiated from the
rest (sometimes referred to as the masses) ; it is, literally and
etymologically, the chosen or choice part, the "New York cut."
The criteria of selection (or the products of selection) are described by different writers in one or more of three dimensions:

first, the elite exerts (or possesses) crucial *power* with respect to
the decisions in its society, or in that sector of the society in which it is "elite";

second, the elite is the beneficiary of special *privilege* in terms of
wealth, income, and/or other perquisites;
third, the elite has high *prestige* in the society as a whole, and/or
in that sector of the society in which it is elite.[14]

Early writings and some modern works on the subject equate
the elite with a ruling minority class, or with a chosen sector
of such a class—the select of the select. Such an interpretation
of course assumes a stratified society in which there is a more
or less definite, bounded, and continuing ruling class. Many
recent treatments of modern societies divorce the concept of
elites from that of class and acknowledge the possibility of
entrance into the elite from several social strata. Early writings
tended also to identify social and political power with wealth,
social privilege, and prestige in the elite group. Since the
Great Depression, it has been clear that in this country wealth
is a guarantor neither of power nor of prestige. And contrary
to Thorstein Veblen's theses about the leisure class, which ap-
proximated the concept of elite, it is also clear that elitism, in
terms of power, is not necessarily rewarded with leisure, with
income, or with great prestige. Some of our most influential
leaders work long hours, take no vacations, and are under-
paid. In fact, the topmost figures in government are probably
the hardest working and among the relatively least rewarded
in society. Furthermore, membership in a "power elite" is a
risky business; there is no guarantee of tenure in general
elitism.

Recent studies of public decision-making, particularly at
the community level, have made it clear that the "influen-
tials" on different kinds of decisions change, depending upon
the issue at hand. This is to say that the memberships in
"power elites" depend upon the nature of the problem. It is

14. Thirty years ago, Harold Lasswell wrote: "The influential are those who
get the most of what there is to get. Available values may be classified as
deference, income, safety. Those who get the most are *elite;* the rest are *mass.*"
Politics: Who Gets What, When, How (Meridian Books, The World Publishing
Company, Cleveland, 1963), p. 13. (Originally published in 1936 by McGraw-
Hill Book Company.)

doubtful that one could define and delimit any single elite in any community, in any state, or least of all in the national government. Power is fragmented by subject, by profession and occupation, by section, and by jurisdiction.

For these reasons, I am doubtful of the utility of a theory presuming a generalized governing elite to explain the conduct of decision-making in American governments. I doubt the existence, at least in measurable definition, of any "interlocking directorate" in the United States in the terms posed by C. Wright Mills and implicit in the reputational methodology developed by Floyd Hunter. On the other hand, I am convinced of the existence of elites in particular agencies, and with respect to particular types of programs, of American government, whereby dominant influence upon public policy is exerted by a relatively small group of persons, official and non-official, who are acknowledged specialists or professionals in their fields. Our elitism today is based not upon social class or wealth or general wisdom. We have a very great variety of elites in many areas, usually defined in terms of occupational and program specialism and of educational achievement considered relevant to that specialism. We have in an increasing number of individual agencies an elite corps which is unique to, and may be completely unrecognized outside of, the agency concerned. One of the greatest problems of American democracy is the nature of the membership, the control, and the coordination of these multifarious elites.

THE RIGHTS OF PUBLIC SERVANTS

The final issue concerning democracy and the public service to be mentioned here is quite different from the others It concerns the deprivations for individual public servants of rights and privileges which other citizens enjoy, deprivations which are justified on the grounds that they are necessary to assure the continuing viability of the democratic state. The rationale for most if not all of these deprivations is commonly rooted in the concept of sovereignty, meaning essentially su-

premacy: the relations between the sovereign people, through
the mechanism of the state, and its servants cannot be governed by the kinds of rules and practices that pervade the
relations of individual citizens and their employers in the
private sector of society. The sovereign will of the people
must be protected, even though this may mean that the public
servant must sacrifice some benefits he might otherwise enjoy.
"A public job is a privilege, not a right." So runs the argument.

There are four principal kinds of programs which have
operated to restrict the freedom and the rights of some, many,
or all public employees:

first, the *loyalty and security programs,* which have insisted that
        public employees—as well as aspirants for federal jobs
        —be loyal to the national government and have ad-
        mitted as evidences of such loyalty a variety of informa-
        tion as to beliefs, associations, and living habits
second, programs to restrict *political contributions* and certain
        political activities of public employees to assure that
        they not utilize, nor be required to exercise, the spe-
        cial nature of their offices to influence partisan elections
third, measures to ensure that public employees do not engage
        collectively through certain techniques, such as the
        strike, the *boycott,* and even (until quite recently) *col-*
        lective bargaining, in contests with their employer, the
        state
fourth, restrictions on the private, non-governmental interests of
        public employees to assure that their public powers not
        be utilized against the general interest, to enhance their
        private personal interests or other private interests
        which might now or later benefit them—i.e. *conflicts of*
        interest.

In all of the cases cited above, public employees have been
specifically enjoined against practices which to other American citizens are more or less specifically guaranteed by constitution or statute. There is here a curious paradox: while all
of these restrictions are rationalized and defended on the

grounds of democracy—government by and in the interests of the whole people—they operate to deprive up to one-sixth of all employed people of democratic rights. All of these alleged infringements upon democratic rights have been and are under attack in various quarters. In the essays which follow, I treat only one of them—that associated with the rights to organize, bargain collectively, and employ certain weapons against the employer—i.e. the government (in Chapter 6). This is not to derogate the significance of the others. All have been considered in other studies. But the one which today is under most virulent attack and undergoing most extreme change is the third, which has to do with collective action of public employees.

2

Education and the Public Service

SOME HISTORICAL STUDIES undertake broad and sweeping surveys of the evolution of total societies, focusing heavily upon significant events, leaders, and trends. Others are directed to evolution of more or less specific subject areas within societies, such as education, or government, or economy. This has often led to the consideration of the development of a given phase of society with only incidental reference to the interaction of that phase with the total context in which it existed. Some recent writers about the history of education have deplored this practice in histories of education in which, they allege, education and particularly the formalized institutions of education have been treated as more or less separate, exogenous factors—with particular reference to American history.[1] The same difficulty has attended a good part of the writing about governmental and administrative history.

I can hardly aspire in these pages to provide any adequate treatment of the interrelationship of the history of public services with the evolution of societies. But an aspect of that interrelationship has come in recent years to invite inquiry by one interested in the current public services—the interlocking of the evolution of education and that of the public services, particularly of the "elite" personnel at the higher levels. My

1. See particularly Bernard Bailyn, *Education in the Forming of American Society* (New York, Random House, 1960).

own inquiry was stimulated principally by three current considerations:

first, the present-day dependence of the American public service upon the products, in terms both of people and of knowledge, of our educational institutions, particularly at the level of higher education; and the concurrent influence of government upon the educational system, its extent and its directions;

second, the widespread differences among the higher public services of the United States, Great Britain, and continental Europe—despite the fact that all grew from origins and ideologies that were somewhat similar;

third, the discoveries and hypotheses of students of comparative administration of the interdependence of educational systems and their governing elites, particularly in the developing countries.

It is doubtful that there is any element in an evolving culture more significant for the nature of its public service than the educational system, both formal and informal, by which are transmitted its ethos, frames of reference, and knowledge, and partly through which these are changed and knowledge is enlarged. This is not to suggest that the educational system can be viewed as an *independent* variable operating outside of and upon the society or its public service. It is a part of and a respondent to its society; and, as will be shown below, it responds to the demands of public administration while at the same time shaping the nature of that administration. The interdependence of the educational system and the society of which it is a part is a tautology, for the educational system is a principal means whereby the society maintains and transforms itself. Its influence upon government and particularly upon public administration and the public service is immediately reflected in:

1. the degree to which public purposes are directed to the entirety or to special segments of the population;

2. the potential capacity for, and the limits upon, the performance of particular governmental activities;
3. the degree of democratization of the public service in the
limited sense of providing opportunity for responsible
public employment to a larger sector of the society;
4. or, conversely, the degree to which the public service is stratified among particular classes of the population, themselves partly defined in terms of educational attainment;
5. the degree to which the public service can pursue technical
and specialized programs in fields requiring particularized instruction and experience.

In regard to items three and four above, it has long been true,
and it is probably true today in virtually every country of the
world, that there exists a direct relation between the nature
and the level of educational attainment on the one hand and
access to different strata and specializations of positions in the
public service on the other. It is also true, though in widely
varying degree, that there is a relation between an individual's educational attainment and specialization and his economic and social status. In other words, the educational
system provides the intermediary between one's social and
economic status and his level and influence in the society and
its government. In the long pull, change in the direction
either of democratization or of improvement of qualifications
of the public service or both cannot occur without equivalent
and usually prior changes in the educational system. This is to
say, among other things, that the nature and quality of the
public service depend heavily upon the nature of the system
of education.

But the proposition is equally accurate when stated in the
other direction. In modern times at least, the democratization
of education, as well as its nature (in terms of emphasis upon
science, classics, humanities, vocations, etc.), depends heavily
upon public policy and the influence of the public service. In
many, perhaps all, societies the fundamental education is
transmitted through the family or through immediate kin.

But formal and advanced education is very largely the responsibility of public agencies, whether local schools, or intermediary governments, such as the American states and their universities, or nations. Many of the most advanced institutions of higher learning are privately endowed and controlled, but even among them there is an acknowledged public responsibility. Thus, while education determines, augments, and limits the potentialities of public administration, public policy to a substantial extent determines, augments, and limits the potentialities of education. Among modern nations, both democratic and totalitarian, there has generally been public pressure to enlarge the availability of education, to expand its reaches at higher levels, and to influence its development in specific directions of national interest. Among the developing nations, the enlargement of educational opportunities and educational specialization has increasingly been recognized as a primary requisite of modernization.

EUROPEAN EXAMPLES

The linkages of social class with education and of education with the public service are nicely reflected in the structures of the public services as they have evolved since feudal days in western Europe. Though there are wide differences in the nature of the personnel systems of the European states, most of them are grounded in certain fundamental premises or traditions:

that the top policy-level posts, though variously defined, should be filled by politically appointed and politically responsive officers;

that the remainder of the public service (except at the custodial, messengerial level) should be career personnel, selected and appointed upon completion of their education with expectation of continuing employment in their working life in the civil service and, frequently, in the agency or ministry in which they are initially appointed;

that the career service personnel should be categorized in four

basic classes, roughly matched with four levels of job
responsibility on the one hand and with classes or strata
of the society, existing now or at some time in the past,
on the other;

that the basic criterion, the minimum qualification, for entry
into each class should be the level of educational attainment, though not necessarily the field of educational
specialization;

that the level of educational attainment is roughly related to the
social class in the society.

The four-class structure is found in most of the leading nations of western Europe—Britain, France, Germany, Italy,
Austria, and Belgium—and with variations, in some of the
others. Each class has its distinctive qualification requirements, salary scale, promotion opportunities, and other familiar elements of personnel administration. Each has its
distinctive levels of duties and responsibilities to perform in
the government, though there are varying degrees of specialization within individual classes. Entry into each is meshed in
general terms with a given level of pre-entry education. To a
surprising extent, the classes in these respects are similar
among the different countries, even though there exist wide
disparities in the philosophy and administration of the public
service. The classes (here designated by their British names),
with their general educational requirements and their kinds
of responsibilities in government work, are as follows: * [2]

| administrative class | university graduation | general direction, policy, advice to ministers |

* The titles of the classes of course differ from country to country, though
they are otherwise comparable. In France, they are simply A, B, C, and D; in
Italy, *carriere direttive, carriere di concetto, carriere esecutive,* and *carriere del
personale ausiliario;* in Germany *höherer Dienst, gehobener Dienst, mittlerer
Dienst,* and *einfacher Dienst.*
2. Based primarily upon Brian Chapman, *The Profession of Government*
(London, George Allen and Unwin, Limited, 1959), pp. 76–7.

executive class	highest level education prior to university	detailed supervision and office management
clerical class	completion of first major school examinations (age about 16)	clerical, mechanical, routine
messengerial class	primary school	messengers, porters, chauffeurs, etc.

American students may be reminded of the division of the U.S. civil service system into "services," which were abolished by the Classification Act of 1949. The old services included: (P) Professional and Scientific; (SP) Subprofessional; (CAF) Clerical, Administrative, and Fiscal; (CU) Custodial; and Clerical-Mechanical. Each had its own salary scale, though they were to some extent aligned with each other. But it is interesting, and probably significant of the differences between European and American views of the public service as far back as 1923 when the services were set up, that the prestigious field was professional, not administrative. The respect accorded administrative work was such that it was clustered with clerical and fiscal and, in fact, listed after clerical.

The structure of the career civil services of European states mirrors the stratification of the society in the past and, to some degree, reinforces it. Limiting the top class of career servants, who had and still have the greatest influence on public policy and program, to graduates of universities restricted the access to influential public positions to those social and economic groups which could afford a university education. Opportunities for university education were, until very recently, extremely restricted in Europe as they had been in the United States until the middle of the nineteenth century. The class structure of the civil services assured dominance in administration by persons from the upper class of society (which itself of course might, and indeed did, change in its constituencies). To some extent, the system did and probably still does provide a built-in motivation for conservatism, the maintenance of the social *status quo*. Under the social pressure toward egalitarianism—meaning here the equalization of opportunity—and of governmental need in time of crisis, particularly war and fear of war, the stringencies of the structural barriers in the civil services were relaxed somewhat. New devices were inaugurated for the employment of specialists and professionals in fields other than the "profession of government"; opportunities for advancement from a lower to a higher civil service class were opened, though often on a temporary basis and usually with substantial restrictions.

But in the long pull the most important element toward "democratizing" the European public services has been, and no doubt will continue to be, the democratizing of higher education through public universities and fellowship programs whereby students who lack financial resources, and who come from the lower social strata, may be educated. This trend toward democratization of the public service has been observable in Britain, France, and some other European nations since World War II, though its manifestations and its pace have differed widely. The vital point is that such democratization as has occurred in the European public services has come about not primarily through modification of the structures of the public services and their entrance requirements, but mostly through modification of the educational system—its enlargement, its relaxation of social and economic requirements for admission, its financial support. Most of these changes have been state-induced and state-supported.

Yet there are very considerable differences among the public services of the European states, and these differences reflect the varying developments of their educational systems. In Britain, the administrative class was clearly tailored, about a century ago, to the qualities and intellectual qualifications of the products of its two great universities, Oxford and Cambridge. And for the most part it continues to reflect that bias today. The emphasis in this basic education was upon the classics and the humanities, modified in recent decades, particularly at Cambridge, with mathematics and the hard sciences. The recruiting and examining systems for the administrative class were designed to select from among the best of the products of these schools with rather little regard to the nature of their responsibilities if appointed to the public service. This was, and continues to be, a recruitment system based upon and tailored to an elite educational system which quite deliberately accepted the content and criteria of the educational structure as qualifying for administrative appointment in the government. It had the effect, of course, of prejudicing against entry into the higher reaches of the public service students and others experienced in the professions such as law and medicine and engineering, and students of the social sciences such as economics and government and sociology. The administrative class in Britain today remains predominantly a group of gentlemen, the majority of whom are products of the public schools (in the United States, read private schools) and most of whom are steeped in the classical and scientific curricula of Oxford and Cambridge.[3] It is virtually uncontaminated by lawyers, engineers, educators, business administrators, economists, and other specialists. It represents in one sense the purest profession of governmental administrators, for it is specifically equipped for little else. On the other hand, some would doubt that it qualifies as professional at all since there is little relationship between its pre-entry educational requirements and the activities it is called upon to perform. The British administrative class may perhaps best be described as a group of dedicated and perhaps highly capable "professional amateurs."

3. For a fascinating review of the relationships between the British educational tradition and its administrative class, see Rupert Wilkinson's *Gentlemanly Power: British Leadership and the Public School Tradition* (London, New York, Oxford University Press, 1964).

For present purposes, however, it is unnecessary to evaluate the British administrative class or the system whereby it is sustained. The main point is that it provides a striking illustration of the interdependence of the educational system and the nature of the public service. Revolutionary changes in education are under way in Britain today—as an outgrowth of the Robbins report [4] among other things—and very probably they will occasion revolutionary changes in the British public service. But it should be noted even here that the interaction goes both ways. The Robbins Commission was established by the government, and most of its recommendations call for, or rely upon, governmental action and support. Government, in response to social, political, and international pressures, brings about changes in the public and private educational systems, and these changes, over a longer stretch of time, bring about changes in the constituency of government itself.

On the Continent developed an approach which we would today describe as more pragmatic than the British. It rested on the proposition that there are certain kinds of knowledge and subject matter which are appropriate and indeed requisite for the public official and that these may be provided by universities and other institutions of higher learning. Views as to what is the proper educational content of university programs preparatory for top positions in the public service varied in different countries and evolved over time in somewhat different ways. Most famous was the development in seventeenth- and eighteenth-century Prussia and Austria of *cameralism,* a system of higher education and merit system management designed to staff the higher civil service with men trained in what was then seen as the "stuff" of administration in a monarchical state. Chairs in cameralistics were established in a few German universities, and admissions to examination for the higher public service were for a brief

---

4. Report of the Committee on Higher Education, appointed by the Prime Minister and chaired by Lord Robbins, *Higher Education* (London, Her Majesty's Stationery Office, reprinted 1965).

period limited to graduates of programs in cameralism. The subject itself comprised those fields considered essential to the efficient management of a highly centralized, paternalistic state in an economy of mercantilism. They included predominantly what we would today refer to as public finance, including both revenue and expenditure administration, police science, and economics, with particular emphasis upon agriculture.[5] In some ways, cameralism was the principal precursor of the development of public administration in the United States in the first half of the present century, even though it had been virtually dead in Germany and Austria for nearly a century. A number of the early American apostles of public administration training had studied in Germany and were influenced by the earlier German experience with cameralism, and by its subject-matter successors: political economy, administrative theory, political theory, and the beginnings of the social sciences in general.

Cameralism as a system of thought and as a method of training for public service was gradually and almost completely displaced during the latter part of the eighteenth and the first part of the nineteenth centuries by the field of law. The shift in Germany and Austria from the cameralistic to the legal approach was so profound, so extreme, and, in historic terms, so rapid as to make one wonder as to its causes. Friedrich attributed it to a variety of factors: the emergence of constitutionalism and legalism to regularize the relations between states and citizens and to protect the freedom and property of the individual; the absorption of the judiciary by the monarchs; the replacement of mercantilism by the laissez-faire economics of Adam Smith and his followers; the codification of law, first in Austria, then in Germany, then under Napoleon in most of continental Europe; the conquest by the

5. According to Carl Friedrich, cameralism was also profoundly influenced by political, particularly Aristotelian, theory, the state and its bureaucracy becoming the principal agent for achieving the "common good." "The Continental Tradition of Training Administrators in Law and Jurisprudence," *The Journal of Modern History,* June 1939, XI, 2, p. 131.

monarchs of the feudal estates; the growth of administrative, quasi-judicial tribunals; the personal predilections of individual monarchs; and others.[6]

In consequence of this shift, the content of training for the higher public service became dominantly legal, oriented not to the efficient management of the king's estate but to the proper application of law and due process. For the higher public services in Europe today, preparation remains primarily the study of law, and the great majority of administrative leaders are lawyers. It should be noted, however, that a law program in most European universities is typically broader in scope than in England or in most law schools of the United States. It normally includes some work in what we term social science, such as economics, political science or philosophy, and sociology. Legal training for public administrators is defended not only because there is need of legal skills but also because such an education is believed to provide the habits of thought and frame of mind required by the administrative generalist. Yet, the monopolization of the higher civil services by legally trained officials significantly reflects a particular kind of view of the state and its role in the society as well as a particular kind of concept of the content of public administrative work. At the same time, it induces and probably perpetuates a legal method and style of decision-making and of performance in public administration. The nature of this style and method is perhaps epitomized in the view, which is widely held in Germany, Italy, and some other countries, that the desirable preparation and the initial qualifications of judges and administrators are essentially comparable.[7] It is reflected in the heavy reliance, in most European ministries, upon legal codes, rules, regulations, and precedents. It is reflected in some of Max Weber's writings about legitimate bureaucracy, an

6 Ibid. pp. 130–47.

7. See, for example, Chapman's discussion of this topic, op. cit. Chapters 2 and 3.

idealized type which undoubtedly drew heavily upon his observations and conceptions of the German civil service.

France, with its Napoleonic rule in the early nineteenth century, its legal codification, its Conseil D'Etat, its highly centralized and rationalized administrative structure, probably had as much to do with the development of the legal tradition in the higher civil service as any other nation. Yet France never placed such exclusive reliance upon law as some other countries did, and in recent decades it has been moving farther away from it. Well before the French Revolution (in 1747) the French established two of its famous technical schools, the Ecole Nationale des Ponts et Chaussées and the Ecole Nationale Supérieure des Mines, and soon after the Revolution (in 1794) they created the Ecole Polytechnique. These institutions have long been renowned for their high quality of training of engineers, scientists, and technicians, both for the military and civil services and, indeed, for private employment. All of these schools are state-owned and are operated primarily to provide the state a supply of technicians who are also qualified for posts of higher management. Two years of basic scientific training in the Ecole Polytechnique is normally prerequisite for the three-year curriculum of either of the others, and these latter two are the principal suppliers to the higher civil services of the engineering and technical ministries. Until the close of World War II, entry to the most responsible non-technical posts in the French civil service— i.e. the "grands corps" (Cour des Comptes, Conseil d'Etat, and Inspection Générale des Finances) was restricted to university graduates who attained a diploma from the Ecole Libre des Sciences Politiques, a private institution with prohibitively high fees. This effectively limited recruitment to the wealthy classes.

Comprehensive reforms, intended among other things to "democratize" the "grands corps" and the higher civil service generally, were instituted in 1946-47. Most celebrated among these reforms was the establishment of the Ecole Nationale d'Aministration (ENA) as the sole recruiting and selecting agency for the higher civil service (other than the technicians). It was also to provide a three-year post-entry program of training and supervised experience for prospective civil servants prior to assumption of a regular government post. Applicants for admission must have graduated from a university and most of them must have specialized in the kinds of humanistic and social subjects treated in the stiff ENA entrance examinations.[8] Training in the ENA itself is at the post-graduate level in a fairly broad spectrum of fields considered appropriate for higher civil servants. Law, and particularly administrative law, receives less emphasis in the ENA examinations and in its own curricula than in some other European countries. But the legal content is there, and the legal orientation of French administration is substantial, certainly in comparison with either the British or the American governments. The most prestigious and probably still the most influential of the "grands corps" is the Conseil d'Etat; and its *pièce de résistance,* indeed its reason for existence, is administrative law. The legal approach dominates others of the "grands corps" and the ministries which they administer, such as finance and even the government of the civil service itself.

Yet the ENA represents a radical departure in Europe and a significantly different approach in the relations between the educational system and the higher public service, one which has given rise to a number of somewhat different kinds of experiments in education for the higher civil services of Europe —as at Speyer in Germany and Bologna in Italy. Its effectiveness in moving toward the objective of democratizing the higher public service has, according to recent studies, been less than spectacular; progress has at best been gradual and moderate. The bulk of successful candidates still come from the upper classes, mainly in Paris where the strongest univer-

8. Although some in lower divisions of the civil services are permitted to take the examination.

sity exists. As in all the other European countries, even including Britain, democratization of the higher public service, as the term is used in this chapter, depends basically upon extending and enlarging the opportunities for higher education, and this depends initially upon educational opportunities at lower levels. This is true in the United States as well.

The foregoing paragraphs indicate the distinguishing aspects of the higher public services in principal European countries and show, in each case, their close interconnection with the system of higher education. They fall in three main classes: the British, with its allegiance to the Oxbridge and public school tradition and its "professional-amateur" administrative class; the continental (except the French) with its heavy emphasis upon law; and the French, with its long-standing institutions for post-entry instruction in technical fields, and its more recent efforts to generalize, standardize, and equalize both its selection and its training processes for the "grands corps." All grew, in widely differing ways, from feudal and monarchical origins. Until quite recent times, all maintained effective dominance by the upper middle and upper classes of the higher public services, primarily through the intermediacy of their respective systems of higher education. And all have in recent years, more particularly since World War II, been the objects of reform efforts, primarily in three directions:

first, to democratize their higher civil service by opening its gates of entry to larger segments of the population, principally through democratizing higher education;

second, to strengthen their capacities to deal effectively with the social, economic, political, and technological problems in a period of accelerating change through, for example, bringing in to responsible positions persons educated in a variety of professional, scientific, and technical fields —in addition to law;

third, to enlarge their capabilities in the areas of administration, management, and, broadly, politics.

The steps taken or proposed in all three of these directions in Europe depend partly upon changes within the anatomy of the public services themselves, but over the long pull they depend most upon modifications of the educational systems. It is interesting, parenthetically, that these same three subjects have been principal targets of criticism and reform among the older *career systems* in the United States, such as the military services and the Foreign Service (see Chapter 5 below).

The systems of higher public service described above have of course had an influence going far beyond the shores of Europe. They have provided the beams and girders of most of the bureaucracies of the world—through military and then civil occupation, through colonization, and through a peaceful process of international osmosis consisting of technical assistance and advice, imitation, and education in one of the institutions of a European country, whether it was Oxford or Cambridge, the Sorbonne, Berlin, Bologna, or, more recently, Moscow. For better or worse, the public service systems of Europe and the educational foundations on which they are based have left an indelible impress upon most of the modernizing world. The military and civil services of most of the developing nations which were once European colonies are a mixed, sometimes mixed-up, product of the imposition of the public service concepts of the imperial country upon native traditional and tribal institutions. The stamp of the British administrative class concept continues in most of those lands which once were colored red in the atlases. And the stamp of legalism remains strong in those lands once held by continental countries. That this process did not require occupation or colonization is illustrated in the Prussian influence on the development of the Japanese governmental institutions and the British and French on that of Thailand.

The American Experience

The differences between the American civil services today and their counterparts in Britain or France or Germany are, if anything, more striking than the differences among the three European countries which have been described above. The evolution of our education-public service systems is particularly interesting in this regard because, through a substantial part of our history, the principal exogenous influences upon our development were specifically England, France, and Germany in approximately that historical order. Most of the early Americans were of course themselves transplanted Englishmen who brought with them the culture, the mores, and the institutions which they had grown up with. Later we were significantly influenced by and to a considerable extent dependent upon the French, particularly for engineers and technicians. Still later, our ideas about education and about public administration were heavily influenced from Germany. Yet the product, in respect both to the educational system and to the public service, is unique, one might almost say indigenous. And increasingly during the twentieth century, the flow of influence has been in the direction of America to Europe rather than Europe to America in regard to both the educational system and the public service system.

The base from which colonial America started was purely that of the mother country. After some early and largely frustrating attempts to "civilize" the natives, our forebears did not undertake to rule them, or to educate them, or to accommodate to their institutions. They pursued the simpler (and altogether disgraceful) expedient of driving them west and in the process exterminating a great portion of them. There were of course gaping differences among the colonists in their cultural heritages and their attitudes—the Puritans in New England, the great planters in the South, the yeomen farmers in the mid-Atlantic states and, to some extent in both north and south, the gradually growing numbers of traders, merchants, and craftsmen in the seaboard cities. Yet, in its basic characteristics, the social system which framed the patterns of education in their broad dimensions was essentially similar to that of the mother country. The dominant element was the family, a patriarchal institution which, through kinship relationships and largely immobile geographic and vocational patterns, extended its influences to the community and its governmental institutions. Through the family were transmitted the basic values of the society, the approved patterns of behavior, the approved manners, mores, and view of the world. In addition the family, in medieval Britain and early America, provided the basic and sometimes the only occupational and vocational education for the young. The community in which the family resided provided a second level of education, hardly separable, however, from the family with which it was closely related. The church provided the third major institution of education, partly through schools but also, with or without formal schooling, through the inculcation of moral and spiritual values and through the unifying influence of organized religion upon social integration.

An early device of more advanced vocational instruction, developed in Great Britain and continued in America, was the apprenticeship, whereby young persons were contracted out for extended periods for training in given fields, under conditions of relationship basically comparable with that of the patriarchal family: the master assumed the role and the responsibilities of the father in return for training the appentice in a given craft or trade or even profession. These institutions—the family, the community, the church, and the practice of apprenticeship—were in medieval England and in early America the primary mechanisms of education in its broadest sense—the transmission of culture and knowledge. They were augmented to a growing but limited degree by formal systems of instruction in schools and universities. These institutions, however, were available only to the few— in the universities to a tiny minority, principally individuals preparing themselves for the ministry. Formal education in neither the old country nor the new was a governmental enterprise except in a spasmodic and indirect way. For the most part it was sponsored and supported by the church, by private philanthropy, and by the communities. It is interesting to note that formalized education as it developed in medieval England and was brought to the American colonies was promoted and defended because of its utilitarian services to the society of the day, not because of its broad cultural contributions. The "three R's" and elementary accounting were becoming increasingly essential, at least among a minority of population. And study in the classics and Latin and Greek in the universities was essential in the training of clerics and of the increasing numbers of sons of the gentry (especially under the British primogeniture system which caused so many second and third sons to seek public positions in the Army, Navy, and civil service). From the beginnings of the American colonies, the influential positions in our colonial public services were largely filled from upper classes who had some basis of formal education and a few of whom at least were educated at the university level in the classic subjects dominant at the English universities. This trend persisted for many generations in this country.

It is now clear that the historical bases of American education had been fundamentally modified during the colonial period to the point that, by the time of the American Revolution, we were clearly embarked on a different path, one which would in subsequent decades sharply differentiate our public services (with a few exceptions) from those of our British forebears. Bernard Bailyn, in his perceptive interpretation of the pre-Revolutionary transformation in American education, attributes the changes to "the great axles of society—family, church, community, and the economy. . . ." [9] Basic to his thesis is the breakdown of the extended, patrilineal family which had been brought from the "old country" and which had been predominant in basic education, not only in the teaching of the elementary subjects but more broadly in the transmission of culture from generation to generation in a stable and relatively immobile society. Under the pressure of

9. Bernard Bailyn, op. cit. p. 45.

the demands and perils of wilderness environment and a
marginal economy, the family broke into relatively smaller,
conjugal elements, each self-reliant and independent, few able
to provide the young with the education and the security of
former times. During the same period, the apprentice system,
likewise inherited from England, underwent great stress and
abuse and gradually disintegrated as an educational tool.
Young apprentices had in effect been indentured out to the
masters, who were obligated to take them into their families
and to provide basic education as well as training in a craft.
But with the scarcity of labor, apprentices were increasingly
used as workmen and the educational obligation was ne-
glected. Early colonial laws attempted to enforce both family
and master obligations for education but without notable
success.

Increasingly the colonials had to rely upon formal schooling, often conducted by the local church or the local minister.
But the traditional means of financing schools—principally
private donations and endowments, sometimes supplemented
by tuition—proved insufficient, and gradually the schools had
to turn to the community for contributions and ultimately to
taxation for support. By the close of the colonial period, the
impetus toward a general system of free public schooling,
tax-supported and locally controlled, was well under way. It
was a response to and a part of a broad social transformation
from a tightly knit, localized society in which various elements
were mutually supportive to one in which the individual must
face, virtually alone, the abrasions of a harsh economy and a
frontier environment, yet strove to pass along to his progeny
such cultural and educational advantages as he had. Early
American education was heavily religious, tied to one or
another denomination, but it was also heavily utilitarian in
the sense of preparing the young for vocational usefulness and
advancement. The drive toward universal public education,
which was one of the most prominent features of the nineteenth century and which persists, not quite fulfilled, to this

day, was thus begun well before the American Revolution and was not seriously affected by that event. It made possible and probably hastened the drive toward egalitarianism which we associate with the Jacksonians and the accompanying doctrine that anyone (with the minimum formal education) could perform an adequate job in the civil service.

The momentum toward the egalitarian ideal contrasted sharply with the quite different character of development of higher education. For the pattern, the curricular content, and the faculties of the American colleges were singularly impervious to change until the latter half of the nineteenth century. The early American colleges—there were nine at the time of the Revolution and about twenty-five by 1800— were modeled upon their English predecessors, Oxford and Cambridge. Their offerings heavily emphasized theology, philosophy, the classics, and classical languages. There was rather little of what we would today describe as science and scientific investigation; and there was little vocational or professional training. Both we and the British seem to have forgotten that the medieval European universities were predominantly professional schools, directed to the "learned professions" of the ministry, law, and medicine. Most of the early American colleges were, in a sense, professional, since many of their graduates went into the ministry, and their college training had a heavily ecclesiastical flavor. Others went into other professions, but their college training was hardly directed to this end. Professional training, including legal, was largely provided by apprenticeship.

Until the second quarter of the nineteenth century, attendance was limited principally to well-to-do children in the landed or merchant aristocracies; higher education was a monopoly of the upper class. Although some colleges aspired to attract middle- and lower-class citizens through scholarship programs, these do not appear to have been very successful; even with the scholarships, the fees were beyond the reach of the vast majority. It has been estimated that by 1800 fewer than 10,000 Americans—about two in every thousand—had been to college. By 1828, when Jackson was elected President, the number had more than doubled, but so had the population and the proportion of college graduates to population remained about the same.[10] Yet, from this tiny pool were drawn the majority of persons appointed to the top positions in the federal service, up until and including the appointments of Andrew Jackson.

During the century following the American Revolution, there was an accelerating proliferation of private colleges. Most of them were denominational, and their founding was pushed by both the various churches and the states and communities of their location. They were pushed also by the drive toward egalitarian democracy, with its corollary that young men and, later, women and even Negroes of ability should have an opportunity for a college education. But until the Civil War there was rather little change in the concept of what the mission of the college was or, consequently, in the nature of its curriculum. There were few or no "majors," elective courses, or research, and little of what we would now call graduate work. Subject matter remained theology, philosophy, and classics with a very few significant invasions of the sciences. One consequence was the relative backwardness of American higher education in science until quite recently. A second was the separation of professional education from other higher education. The former was forced to develop through apprenticeship and later through proprietary professional schools, outside the mainstream of higher education.

The reluctance of higher education to support either science or the professions very likely contributed to the Jacksonian egalitarian philosophy of the public service. A college education was not essential to a public job, since a college education did not prepare one for any specialty. It provided culture for a gentleman, but culture was not requisite for public service. The reluctance of American colleges in the

10. Sidney H. Aronson, *Status and Kinship in the Higher Civil Service* (Cambridge, Harvard University Press, 1964), pp. 122-3.

nineteenth century to prepare their students for professional and administrative work, coupled with the Jacksonian denial of careers in the public service, may well have been the death knell of any administrative class in the United States. At the same time, the conservatism of the colleges produced a vacuum which contributed to tremendous counter-movements after the Civil War.

Three major developments in the second half of the nineteenth century had fundamental influence on the subsequent development of education and the nature of the public service. One was the passage of the Morrill Act in the midst of the Civil War, which provided impetus for a host of land-grant state universities dedicated to education in "agriculture and the mechanic arts." The Morrill Act gave expression to the ethos of the nation: equality of opportunity so that most who qualified could gain higher education; faith in knowledge, rationality, and practical research to solve the problems of society; emphasis upon practicality—the study and teaching of subjects which would be helpful in carrying out occupational tasks in agriculture and industry; and a heavy orientation to economic considerations in the subject matter of education. The Morrill Act and the federal and state actions which followed it gave emphasis to the vocational content of higher education; they thus opposed the tendencies prevailing to that date, which were quite plainly anti-vocational. They contributed little immediately to the development of science in the universities except at a rather superficial and applied level. But over time, they provided institutional bases for scientific development and for nexi between the sciences and professional occupations. Finally, they provided the impetus and the bases whereby free, or nearly free, public higher education would later catch up with and surpass private institutions in the numbers of students.

The second major influence on higher education in the latter part of the nineteenth century stemmed from the German emphasis upon science and research and the development of the German universities as institutions for the pursuit and dissemination of knowledge, free of ideological, religious, or political bias and influence. Substantial numbers of American scholars studied in Germany during the middle and later nineteenth century, and they returned with elevated and different standards of knowledge in the various fields of learning, particularly in science. The effects included the emergence of science and research in the higher education scene; the reawakening of scholarship; and the Ph.D. degree, first at Yale (in 1860), later and more importantly at Johns Hopkins (beginning in 1876), which was to become the "union card" for the profession of college-level teaching. They also included profound institutional changes: a tremendous proliferation of subject matter fields and courses; the development of the American style of "university," a mix (which is not fully digested to this day) of the older American patterns of general education of the colleges, the vocational orientation of the land-grant schools, and the emphasis from Germany upon science and research.

A third major influence on higher education was the development, in the latter part of the nineteenth century, of the public high school. Earlier the bulk of college students were in their teens, with little more than an elementary school preparation. Many of the colleges established their own academies to provide at least basic preparatory instruction for college entrance, and a good deal of the materials taught in the colleges, especially the land-grant institutions, were at a level we would today expect to be handled in the high schools. The high school curricula varied from one to four years, and most of them were considered essentially as college preparatory; they were not conceived as terminal programs. "In 1870, for example, eight out of ten high school graduates entered college, where six of them received degrees; there were more than twice as many college graduates in the country as there were people with high school diplomas only." [11] In the years

11. Grant Venn, *Man, Education and Work: Postsecondary Vocational and Technical Education* (Washington, D.C., American Council on Education, 1964), p. 46.

following 1880, the number of four-year high schools grew in geometric progression. By 1920, the number of high school graduates who went on to college fell to about 25 per cent. In short, high school graduation had become terminal for the majority of students. But at the same time, the educational attainment of those who did proceed to college was greatly improved. This in turn made possible the elevation of the level of college instruction. To a very substantial degree, the rapid growth in the depth, the scope, and the numbers enrolled that has occurred in higher education since about 1880 has been made possible by the emergence of the high school.

With the growing support of the high schools, and under the not altogether parallel stimuli of scientism and vocationalism, American higher education burgeoned and assumed its present shape, unique in the world, during the first decades of this century. One most important dimension of this shape was the semi-independent professional school on the university campus. This development reflected—and it also conditioned —some very much larger trends in American society and culture. This was the era of progressivism in politics and of the parallel movement in the field of education also associated with the word "progressive." It witnessed the blossoming of faith in rationality, applied science, and progress. Then was the first vision of the Great Society. Scientific management grew in industry and government, as did conservation and a variety of new applied sciences in agriculture and on the countryside. A hallmark of the period, which continues to this day, was the growth of increasing specialism in the work of the nation, including that of its governments. Specialization was partly spawned and encouraged by the universities through their development of knowledge, partly forced upon them by the demands of society. But specialization on the campuses among both faculties and students became a major prop to occupational specialism on the outside, including, particularly for our purposes, specialism in the public services.

Under the onslaught of social optimism and rationality,

the bastions of traditionalism, the educational institutions, had to yield some ground, though they did not do so without stubborn opposition. Vocationalism penetrated not alone the universities but also the traditional liberal arts colleges and even the public schools. The Smith-Hughes Act of 1917 finally brought federal aid for vocational training below the college level, a full half-century after the Morrill Act had brought it to the universities. Professional and pre-professional educational programs began to appear in the curricula of even the most conservative four-year liberal arts colleges, a movement which has continued to this day. The general view that the educational system should aim toward the preparation of young people for their working lives as well as, or instead of, preparing them for a life of culture, took hold at all levels. The acceptance of professional training on college and university campuses was spotty, sporadic, often reluctant. But the trend was inexorable and resulted in a situation in which the bulk of higher education, undergraduate and graduate, was in fact directed to the preparation of young people for working careers. That is, it became professional.

The early drive toward identifying education and its institutions with work and with current social problems was in some places more pronounced than it is today. In 1899 the University of Chicago, then only six years old, established a college of commerce and politics to deal with, among other things, "the principal economic, social and political problems which confront the leading nations of the world." [12] In keeping with this spirit, Chicago engaged Dr. Edmund J. James as Professor of Public Administration, to my knowledge the first such title in the history of the United States. During the same period, the University of Wisconsin inaugu-

12. Edmund J. James, "Commercial Education" (thirteenth of the *Monographs on Education in the United States*, ed. by Nicholas Murray Butler, Louisiana Purchase Exposition Company; Albany, New York, J. B. Lyon Co., 1899), pp. 40–41.

rated its program of total service to the state and society. Its president, Charles Van Hise, declared in 1905: "I shall never be content until the beneficent influence of the University reaches every family in the state. This is my ideal of a state university." [13] And Wisconsin blazed new trails in its extension program in agricultural and urban affairs, its various programs of social reform, its support of trade unionism, and its institutional economics. During the same decade, the first of this century, the most venerable educational institution in the country was debating a proposal for a professional school to train diplomats and civil servants. The discussions resulted eventually, in 1908, in the Harvard School of Business, the change in focus resulting primarily because of doubts of career possibilities in the diplomatic and civil services.

The invasion of professional education upon university campuses began in earnest at about the same time—that is, about 1900. As late as 1895, Nicholas Murray Butler wrote that the only two professional schools of "university rank" in the United States were Harvard in law and Johns Hopkins in medicine.[14] But profound changes were taking place, changes which would revolutionize higher education in the United States:

1. the rapid development of sciences, both social and physical, which could provide a sound basis for the development of professional training;
2. the transfer of professional education in many fields from proprietary schools and on-the-job apprenticeship to the university campuses;
3. the birth of a number of new professions, mostly spawned on university campuses by providing academic substance to existing vocations (During the first quarter of this century, systematic university training was developed,

13. Quoted in Lawrence A. Cremin, *The Transformation of the School* (New York, Vintage Books, 1964), p. 165.

14. In his introduction to the American version of Friedrich Paulsen, *German Universities: Their Character and Historical Development* (New York, The Macmillan Company, 1895), p. xxv.

for example, in such fields as accounting and business
education, journalism, nursing, optometry; further, during that period a number of professions developed
which were more or less specifically directed to the public service: city planning, city management, diplomacy,
forestry, public health, social work, teaching.);
4. the reform and upgrading of standards of professional education in the older fields—such as medicine and law—as
well as the newer ones and the pushing of educational
requirements up into graduate levels of instruction.

These trends, especially the first, third, and fourth, have
continued to this day. World War II and later Sputnik provided new impetus for them, especially the rapid development of the sciences. With the resulting burst of knowledge
has come the ever-growing tendency, if not the outright
necessity, to intensify specialization, to dig deeper into specialties of specialties of specialties. This has been in part a
consequence of the demands and subventions of the users of
the products of the universities, businesses, and governments;
but in part it also derives from the universities themselves
and from the explosions of knowledge for which they provide the principal fuses.

The growth of professional training on the campuses has
been the largest part of the accelerating growth in higher education in this country. About three-fifths of all degrees
granted in 1964-65 were in professional fields. Another 8 per
cent were in the natural sciences, and most of these degree-
holders proceeded to professional careers. Only one-ninth
were in the humanities, the nineteenth-century staple of
higher education, and a substantial number of these led to
professional careers, principally in teaching. We have, over
the course of the last century, reversed the emphasis and the
directions of higher education: toward vocationalism and
away from humanism; toward specialization and away from
general culture; toward higher education as a right for those
intellectually capable of absorbing it rather than as a privi-

lege for the well-to-do; toward ascription of social status and position on the basis of educational achievement and away from such ascription on the basis of family background and economic resources re-enforced and ratified by higher education.

What are the implications of these developments for the public service and democracy? We are now clearly approaching an early goal of universalization of education at the elementary level for all but a few members of minority groups, even though there remains great unevenness in the quality of such education. We are making substantial progress toward universalization of education at the secondary level, though again with substantial exceptions and inequities. We are moving rapidly toward the objective of higher education for all who are qualified for it, regardless of economic means and social background, and realization of this goal seems possible within the next several decades. In this respect, the United States is clearly far ahead of any other nation, both now and in the long history of civilization.[15]

Higher education has become the principal gateway to upward mobility in our society. As we shall see later, governmental service following such education provides a major channel, once the gate has been passed. At the same time, the increasing emphasis upon degrees and licenses in various professional fields may serve to inhibit such mobility for those still unable to attain higher education. And high educational requirements in different specialized fields probably hinder lateral movement across occupational lines. Relatively high upward mobility provides some assurance of a representative service, in the passive sense.

The movement toward specialization and vocational preparation in higher education and, increasingly, in secondary

15. This assertion refers to the quantitative picture; there may be ground for debate as to the comparative quality and appropriateness of higher education.

education has been mutually supportive of comparable trends in government and industry. A high and rising proportion of public employees are college graduates, specialized and professionally oriented, and they are providing the vast majority of our administrative leadership below the level of political appointments. We have no substantial "administrative class" of cultured gentlemen as in Britain or of legally oriented officials as in continental Europe, and rather little is being done on the campuses to train such a class. Where the problems of most European governments, and those of most of the underdeveloped countries as well, concern the dearth of well-qualified specialists, ours seems to be a surfeit of specialisms and professionals and a glaring need for generalists.

Finally, the growing fractionalization of specialties and the rise of organized professions have given a new cast to the older problems of policy-politics and administration, responsibility, participative democracy, and elitism. The consequences of our recent educational transformation for these issues will be considered in the chapters to follow.

3

The Evolution of American Civil Service Concepts

THE AMERICAN REVOLUTION and its successful separation of the colonies from England did not, any more than most other revolutions, eliminate traditional institutions and mores. Most of them, in the realm of government, were brought over from the "old country" by the colonists; they survived the Revolution, and some continue to this day.[1] The ideology and practice of the early public service of the United States were clearly a heritage of our British forebears. But the Revolution occurred before the great societal and governmental upheavals of Britain and the rest of Europe which came during the late eighteenth and the nineteenth centuries. As has been indicated earlier, nationalist movements, the Industrial Revolution, and the accompanying or closely following drive toward political egalitarianism in Europe had varying, though related, effects upon the governmental systems and public services in European nations. The United States, with its effectual isolation by several thousand miles of ocean, its virtually unlimited western frontier, its vast resources inviting exploitation, and its surging population, could and did go its own way in matters governmental. One consequence was an evolution in the con-

1. E.g. the continuing virility of counties, towns, and villages, and mayors, supervisors, sheriffs, justices of the peace, coroners, grand and petty juries.

cept and practice of its public services entirely different from
that of European countries and, as products of such evolution,
a set of personnel systems which by mid-twentieth century
were unique in the world.

For purposes of summarizing this evolution it is useful to
identify certain key stages in ideology and in practice through
which this country has progressed during its first century and
three-quarters. The dates placed at the beginning and end of
each stage are matters of convenience only; clearly each began before the beginning date assigned, and the influence of
none of them has yet ended. Each made its special contribution to the meaning of "merit" in public employment; and
each added to, and complicated, American concepts as to the
proper nature and role of the public service in a democratic
polity. Indeed, the principal reason for presenting them is
to emphasize their continuing impact upon our values, our
policies, and our practices today.

From the point of view of the public service, I divide our
history into the following arbitrarily bounded periods:

Period	*Benchmark*
1789–1829: government by gentlemen: the guardian period	inauguration of Washington
1829–83: government by the common man: the spoils period	inauguration of Jackson
1883–1906: government by the good: the reform period	Pendleton Act
1906–37: government by the efficient: the scientific management period	New York Bureau of Municipal Research

| 1937–55: government by administrators: the management period | report of Brownlow Committee |
| 1955–: government by the professional: the scientific period | report of Second Hoover Commission |

The paragraphs that follow explore briefly the nature and the principal lasting contributions to concept and practice of the first five of these periods. The latest and current one, government by the professional, is treated separately in Chapter 4.

I. 1789-1829: GOVERNMENT BY GENTLEMEN

Important among the ideological bases of the American Revolution and the subsequent founding of the new government were the goals of egalitarianism among men and of self-government. And important among the devices whereby equality before the government and participation in governmental decisions were to be achieved was representation of the citizenry in the policy-making offices of the government. But the Constitution provided surprisingly little guidance concerning the appointive offices of administration, other than its prescription of appointment by the President and confirmation by the Senate. Washington, the only American president with the opportunity to build an administration "from scratch," was thus substantially free of legal prescriptions and inhibitions, as well as of the burden of past incumbencies and of organized political party pressures. He took this part of his presidential responsibilities with extreme seriousness, and most historians of the period judge his achievements in this area to have been remarkably effective. He set the pattern of appointments to the public service which was to be followed without major change during the first four formative decades of the Republic, and some of its most significant elements survive to this day.

In fact, Washington had rather severe limits upon his freedom, limits imposed by the nature of the society itself. The ringing words of the Declaration of Independence provided objectives and principles rather than descriptions of actuality. "All men" were far from equal in social or economic or political terms. The Congress was "representative" of much less than a majority of the adult males in the population. And the pool from which capable persons could be drawn to operate the administrative machinery of government was minuscule. Over-all, the leadership of the administrative branch during the first quarter of our history was probably considerably less representative of the population as a whole than was the Congress.

The society of the colonies which formed the United States was a heritage of post-feudal, pre-industrial Britain. Farming was the dominant occupation, though business and trade were growing in New England and the middle Atlantic seaboard, and manufacturing, though still on a very small scale, was getting under way. Although we had forbidden the use of titles and other accoutrements of social rank, it was a highly stratified society in which wide gulfs separated the well-to-do, the middling, the poor, and finally the slaves. In a country in which eight to nine out of every ten owed his livelihood to agriculture, the ownership of land was highly concentrated in a few enormous estates, except in New England.[2] The owners of the large estates and plantations, who were a minute fraction of the rural population, constituted the bulk of the aristocracy in the early United States. The largest part of the rural population, however, were middle- and lower-middle-class farmers, owners of modest tracts or tenants, but distinctly separated economically, socially, and politically from the landed gentry.

2. For example, it is reported that three-quarters of the acreage of New York belonged to less than a dozen persons. To the south, the plantation system gradually superseded the earlier yeoman farming. I have relied heavily in this section upon Sidney H. Aronson, *Status and Kinship in the Higher Civil Service* (Cambridge, Harvard University Press, 1964). See his pages 35ff.

Along the seaboard, the social supremacy of the wealthy farm owners was increasingly challenged by a rising urban group of wealthy merchants and traders, itself, however, still a small minority. To these were added a small but growing number of professional men, high in wealth or esteem or both, to complete the constituency of the upper class of early America. Some of the professionals were themselves drawn from the families of the landed gentry. They included principally the clergy, lawyers, doctors, surveyors, college professors, and army officers, but *in toto* they constituted not more than 2 per cent of the labor force in 1800. Clearly, the pecking order of social classes in the early United States was comparable to that in England. And, as in England, its influence penetrated virtually every aspect of American lives —economic, political, social, educational, cultural. The "upper crust" were, for the most part, wealthy and in positions to heavily influence if not dominate those in the lower classes. Despite growing relaxation of suffrage restrictions, they pretty largely controlled the legislative and executive positions and policies of governments in the colonies and later in the states and the nation.

There appears to be general agreement among historians that George Washington and his immediate successors took great pains to assure a high level of competence in their appointments to the principal offices in the executive branch. Washington himself insisted that no considerations other than "fitness of character" should enter into his nominations for public office, and the evidence indicates that in the main this prescription was upheld. But the Federalist merit system necessarily relied upon a special construction of "merit." "Fitness of character" could best be measured by family background, educational attainment, honor and esteem, and, of course, loyalty to the new government—all tempered by a sagacious regard for geographic representation. After Washington came the formation of political parties, and party identification and loyalty played an increasing role in appointments. Yet, in spite of Jefferson's interest in broadening the democratic base of the government, the elite of the administrative group continued to be drawn from the elite of the society in general—from what today might be termed the "establishment." In this regard, as in so many others, we were pursuing the habits of our English forebears. But in sharp contrast with contemporary British practice, our early public service appears to have been remarkably free of corruption, nepotism, and even patronage. The business of governing was prestigious, and it was anointed with high moral imperatives of integrity and honor.

The early public service may be considered to have consisted of two broad categories of personnel. First were those in high-ranking offices who were in the public eye and who exercised significant influence in the making of public policy and had significant responsibility for its execution. They included the Cabinet members and their ranking assistants, overseas ministers, territorial governors, bureau chiefs, chief accountants, and registers of the land offices. Appointed by the President or in a few cases by his department heads, they constituted the elite of the executive branch; they were, in today's terminology, the political executives. The second group were the workers in the offices and the field—the clerks, customs employees, surveyors, postal employees, for example. They corresponded roughly to most of those now covered in the federal civil service system. They were far greater in number, of course, but much less important in shaping the directions of the new government. It should be noted that the great bulk of all employees, and particularly those in the second category, did not work in the Capital but were widely scattered in the states and territories. It has been estimated that as of 1800, all but about 150 of the 3000 federal civilian employees were located in the field.

The two categories were distinctly different, with regard not only to the nature of their responsibilities but also to their social and economic origins and background, their educational attainment, and the nature of their appointments and tenure. The second category, the "workers," came very largely from the middle and upper middle classes. Their work generally required that they have a minimum of elementary education—at least the "three R's." A few had had training or apprenticeship in a profession, such as law or medicine, and some others had specialized backgrounds in accounting or the crafts. Although in the main the members of this group were accorded no statutory or other legal job protection, it seems to have been taken for granted from the very beginning that their tenure was for life or for the duration of their effective service. Removals in this category up to the time of Jackson were limited in number and normally justified by cause. Even under Jefferson and his successor Republican presidents, the practice of "rotation in office" did not take hold for the bulk of the civil service. For this group, the mores and the practice of job security do not appear to have differed substantially from the legally protected security enjoyed by the present-day classified service.

The nature of the membership of the elite group in the federal service during the early period has been the object of much scholarly attention, and the evidence with regard to it is quite substantial. Perhaps the most reliable source is the statistical comparison made by Sidney H. Aronson of appointments of John Adams, Jefferson, and Jackson to elite positions. Aronson's data confirm conclusively the aristocratic nature of the early federal elites. They also indicate that there was only a slight change in the direction of "democratizing" the higher public service by Jefferson in comparison with the Federalists and by Jackson in comparison with the Jeffersonians. Finally, they indicate that the principle and practice of tenure in office did not apply at the top level, particularly when there was a change in party control of the Presidency. Of 87 elite members appointed by Adams, 60, or more than two-thirds, were original appointments—i.e. not holdovers or reappointments from the previous administration. In the case of Jefferson, 73 of 92 elite members, nearly four-fifths, were original appointments; for Jackson, 95 of 108 were original appointments—nearly nine-tenths. The expectancy of job continuity of elite office-holders was on the average less then than it is for the political executives today.

Basing his conclusions primarily upon the occupations of fathers of elite appointees, Aronson shows that the majority of the elites of each of the three presidents came from upper-class families, but at the same time the proportions of upper-class backgrounds declined as between Adams and Jefferson and again as between Jefferson and Jackson. As might be expected from their own backgrounds and geographic residences, Adams relied more heavily upon individuals whose fathers were merchants and professionals than did Jefferson, who accorded greater priority to the sons of the landed gentry.[3]

PRIMARY OCCUPATIONS OF FATHERS OF ELITE MEMBERS

	Adams (N = 100)	Jefferson (N = 104)	Jackson (N = 129)
HIGH-RANKING OCCUPATIONS	%	%	%
Landed Gentry	22	29	21
Merchant	22	13	17
Professional	26	19	15
Total	70	60	53
MIDDLE-RANKING OCCUPATIONS			
Total	23	25	39
UNKNOWN	7	15	8
Grand Total	100	100	100

The dominance of high-ranking occupations among the elite appointees of the three presidents was even more pronounced in consideration of the primary occupations of the appointees themselves. At least 90 per cent of all three groups had been engaged in the top-ranking occupations prior to their appointments, and there were no significant differences among them in this regard. The proportions of appointees in

3. Based upon Aronson, op. cit. p. 61. The middle-ranking category includes artisans, proprietors, farmers, teachers, sea captains, and shop or tavern keepers.

these occupations were for Adams, 92 per cent; for Jefferson, 93 per cent; and for Jackson, 90 per cent. This suggests a substantial and rising degree of upward mobility over the course of time, or a greater disposition on the part of the later presidents to appoint "self-made" men as against those who had inherited high status, or, more probably, some of both.

II. 1829-83: GOVERNMENT BY THE COMMON MAN

The election of Andrew Jackson in 1828 is usually considered a turning point in the direction of American society and its government, the entrance of the society into a new watershed. The "reform" of the public service was only one element of a new egalitarian philosophy of society which contemplated a government "by the people" on the basis of free elections of the masses as well as the well-to-do, and administration by individuals responsive to the electorate either by frequent election or by immediate dependence upon elected officials. The tenets of the spoils system were consistent with the egalitarian ideology and may have been essential to it in the times and circumstances of mid-nineteenth-century America.

As a matter of fact, the attribution of the spoils system—together with its sorry consequences—to President Jackson is less than totally accurate. His own actions and pronouncements with regard to appointments to public office were at least equivocal.[4] In his first inaugural address, he made brief reference to the need of "reform, which will require particularly the correction of those abuses that have brought the patronage of the federal government into conflict with the freedom of elections, and the counteraction of those causes which have disturbed the rightful course of appointments and have placed or continued power in unfaithful or incom-

---

4. The most celebrated statement—and apparently the source of the expression "spoils system"—was made by Senator William L. Marcy of New York in 1832: "They (politicians of the United States) see nothing wrong in the rule, that to the victor belong the spoils of the enemy." (Quoted in Leonard D. White, *The Jacksonians*, New York, The Macmillan Company, 1954, p. 320.)

petent hands." But he followed with a promise to "select men whose diligence and talents will insure in their respective stations able and faithful cooperation, . . ." [5] i.e. men who had a combination of merit and political loyalty. A few months later, in his first annual message to the Congress, he provided a more extended rationale for rotation in office and patronage appointments which included virtual elimination of the merit consideration. He deplored the effects of long tenure in office, the idea of "right to official station," and the view of office as "property." But perhaps most important was the doctrine of the simplicity of public work, a doctrine which we have not fully discarded to this day: "The duties of all public offices are, or at least admit of being made, so plain and simple that men of intelligence may readily qualify themselves for their performance; and I can not but believe that more is lost by the long continuance of men in office than is generally to be gained by their experience." [6]

Yet Jackson's appointments reflected no less concern about ability and competence than did those of his predecessors. While, as noted earlier, a somewhat smaller proportion of his appointees to top level positions were drawn from established upper-class families, he depended equally upon educated and capable men. His efforts to democratize the public service—to make it more representative of the entire population—were only moderately successful because the pool of qualified men was still limited. Actually, the percentage of office-holders whom he removed following John Quincy Adams was very nearly the same as that of Jefferson's removals following Adams's father. Clearly Jackson did not always follow what he sometimes preached.

Jackson's view of public office as a central tenet of an egalitarian philosophy nevertheless became a symbol and guide for his colleagues and successors, not alone at the national

5. James D. Richardson, *Messages and Papers of the Presidents,* Vol. II (Bureau of National Literature and Art, 1903), p. 438.
6. Ibid. p. 449.

level of government but in the states and local units as well. Among the consequences of the spoils system, run rampant, were: the periodic chaos which attended changes in administration during most of the nineteenth century; the popular association of public administration with politics and incompetence; the growing conflicts between executive and legislature over appointments, which led in 1868 to the only attempt to impeach an American president; the almost unbelievable demands upon presidents—and executives of state and local governments as well—by office-seekers, particularly following elections, which were capped by the assassination of a president; the development of political machines in states, counties, and cities (where most government actually was); and the rise to pre-eminence of lawyer-politicans in every branch of government and at every level.

The egalitarian drive which spurred and rationalized the spoils system proved decreasingly effective as a guarantor of popular direction and control of administration. Jackson and his successors reduced the influence of the old aristocracy and opened the gates of public service to the common people. But the new criteria for appointment produced administrations little more representative of the whole people than before, and they made more effectively possible than before decision-making behind the scenes—"invisible government" as it was called. Our public administration at the close of the nineteenth century thus was little more *responsible,* in the sense of being answerable to the whole people, than it had been at the close of the eighteenth century. Nor was it more *responsive* to popular needs and interests. We had effectively though not completely transferred governmental power from one group (the gentry) to another (the politicians); in the process, we suffered a considerable degradation of public office and widespread corruption. We also planted the seeds for a kind of civil service reform quite different from that instituted by Andrew Jackson.

III. 1883-1906: Government by the Good

Despite the sorry practices which led up to it and despite the evangelical fervor of its advocates, the reform of the civil service, marked by the passage of the Pendleton Act in 1883, by no means represented a complete reversal of American practice and ideology vis-à-vis public employment. It signaled a second change in direction, a change which became increasingly significant in the decades which followed; but it built upon the base which prevailed at the time, a base importantly influenced by the Jacksonian period. It did not abolish it and start anew, nor did it undertake to return to the system of the Federalists. On the contrary, civil service reform accepted the principles of egalitarianism and of equal opportunity in the public service. It sought another kind of criterion for personnel administration, which would at the same time continue to assure widespread access to public office among the citizenry. The impetus to civil service reform in this country did not derive from an effort to break a social class monopoly on the public service or to transfer civil service control from one class to another, as it had in Britain and has in many European countries up to very recent years. Though the war for an open public service continues here to this day, the main battles had been won—at least in ideological terms.

The Pendleton Act climaxed one of the most vigorous and spirited reform campaigns in American history. Protests against the spoils system had begun almost as soon as it was given a name, and efforts were made during the 1850's to require qualifying examinations for appointments, particularly to clerical positions. Taking shape in the years following the Civil War, the reform movement commanded the attention of an increasing number of public spirited civic leaders, including many in high political office.[7] Following an abortive

7. The prominence of the leadership of the reform campaign, many of whom considered correction of the spoils system the principal problem of the

attempt by President Grant in 1871 to set up a civil service system, civil service reform grew to become a major political issue in the late seventies and early eighties. The enthusiasm and the dedication which the movement came to command may perhaps best be explained by the fact that its essence was *moral* at a time when American thinking was heavily moralistic. Few reform movements in American history could draw so clear a distinction between right and wrong, between the "good guys" and the "bad guys." It was a campaign *against evils* that were clear and obnoxious.

Three interrelated consequences of the nature of the campaign that led to civil service reform may be noted. First, it associated what we now refer to as personnel administration with morality, with a connotation of intrinsic "goodness" vs. "badness," quite apart from the purposes for which people were employed or the nature of the responsibilities they would carry. Second, although some protagonists mentioned efficiency as an argument for a merit system, this was at best a secondary consideration—"and not a very close second at that," to quote Paul P. Van Riper's analysis of the movement.[8] Third, it was essentially a negative movement designed to stamp out a system which was a "disgrace to republican institutions" [9]—to eradicate evil. There was not very much original thought about the best kind of substitute for spoils beyond competitive entrance examinations and security of tenure. Personnel administration had not yet been invented.

The Pendleton Act was inspired by the British civil service reforms which had followed the Northcote-Trevelyan re-

country at the time, is suggested by the names of Carl Schurz, George William Curtis, Dorman Eaton, John Jay, Richard Henry Dana, and Thomas Jenckes. Leaders during the generation following the Pendleton Act included Theodore Roosevelt and Woodrow Wilson.

8. In his *History of the United States Civil Service* (Evanston, Illinois, Row Peterson and Company, 1958) , p. 85.
Economy and Efficiency, *The Administrative State* (New York, The Ronald Press, 1948), pp. 192ff.

9. As quoted in Waldo, op. cit. p. 192, from Dorman B. Eaton's *Civil Service Reform in Great Britain* (1879).

port. But the products of the adaptation—the Act and its implementation—were more American than British, and they had greatly to do with the kinds of civil services we have today. We accepted from the British the concept of competitive examinations for entrance to public office, though the idea was not altogether new in our government. We also accepted the principle of political neutrality for civil servants, which promised a stable and continuous administrative service free of partisan pressures, obligations, and removal. But even these elements which we adopted in principle we modified with our indigenous stamp. We did not divide our service into a series of scalar classes comparable to the British four-class system and, indeed, never seriously contemplated it. By two significant actions taken on the Senate floor during debate on the bill, we struck down the central tenets of the closed career system implicit in the British model. The first was the insertion in the bill of a requirement that examinations be "practical in character"—i.e. not scholarly, essay-style exercises based upon academic learning but, at least by implication, tests related immediately to the requirements of the job to be filled. An incidental effect of this provision was to lay the basis for the development some decades later of a detailed system of position classification. Examinations could be made truly "practical" only if the positions to be filled were analyzed, described, and related to the knowledges and skills required for their performance. Secondly, the Senate struck out a requirement that entrance be permitted only "at the lowest grade." It was to be an "open" civil service with no prohibition of what we now call lateral entry. There was provided no linkage between the entrance system and the products of any particular universities, as in Britain, nor was there a linkage to the products of universities in general. In fact, the bias was in quite the opposite direction. In 1905, the Civil Service Commission in its *Twenty-Second Report* stated that ". . . the greatest defect in the Federal Service today is the lack of opportunity for ambitious, well-educated young men."

It was not until the 1930's that, through the efforts of Commissioner Leonard D. White and the National Institute of Public Affairs, this lack began to be remedied.

Nor did we very thoroughly emulate the British in the matter of neutrality. For while we did endeavor to insulate civil servants from the hazards of patronage and political pressures—and while we have since strengthened the protections and inhibitions—we did not contemplate that those insulated would be in positions to direct the operations of whole agencies. We established no administrative class, no "permanent undersecretaries." Political and policy direction in the administration continued to rest in the President, his politically appointed secretaries, and the political appointees of both, none of them protected by civil service regulations. Civil service protection pushed sporadically upward in the hierarchy, but to this day the top levels are filled by political appointees who number in the hundreds, even in the thousands if one liberally defines the leadership jobs.

The concept of neutrality gave the early enthusiasts for civil service reform difficulties, even as it continues to give difficulties today. How can a public service which is neutral in political matters and which is protected be responsive to a public which expresses its wishes through the machinery of elections and political parties? There is no reason to doubt that the proponents of civil service reform were as vigorous in their support of popular control of government as their Jacksonian predecessors, and very likely they were just as fearful of an "entrenched bureaucracy." A possible intellectual escape from this dilemma resided in the doctrine of the separation of politics and policy from administration. I call it an "intellectual escape" because I doubt that it had any more empirical basis in the 1880's than it has today, if as much. Policy is determined by the elective representatives of the people—the legislators, the chief executive, and his politically appointed and accountable assistants; administration is the neutral execution of this policy by a competent, continuing administrative corps. It seems significant that Woodrow Wilson, an ardent advocate of civil service reform and later a president of the National Civil Service Reform League, made the most vigorous statement on this dichotomy to that date in his remarkable essay, "The Study of Administration," in 1887, only four years after the Pendleton Act.[10]

Wilson saw administrative reform as the necessary sequel to civil service reform: ". . . we must regard civil-service reform in its present stages as but a prelude to a fuller administrative reform. We are now rectifying methods of appointment; we must go on to adjust executive functions more fitly and to prescribe better methods of executive organization and action. Civil-service reform is thus but a moral preparation for what is to follow." Then he enlarged on the political neutrality theme: "Let me expand a little what I have said of the province of administration. Most important to be observed is the truth already so much and so fortunately insisted upon by our civil service reforms; namely that the administration lies outside the proper sphere of *politics*. Administrative questions are not political questions. Although politics sets the tasks for administration, it should not be suffered to manipulate its offices." This point, the apolitical nature of public administration, was the theme most stressed and probably best remembered: [11] "The field of administration is a field of business. It is removed from the hurry and strife of politics; it at most points stands apart even from the debatable ground of constitutional study. It is a part of political life only as the methods of the counting-house are a part of the life of society; only as machinery is part of the manufactured product."

10. Woodrow Wilson, "The Study of Administration," *Political Science Quarterly* (June 1887), pp. 197–222.
11. Though, as Waldo has noted, there appears to be some inconsistency in the essay on the point. In his first paragraph, Wilson had described as the first object of administrative study to discover "what government can properly and successfully do," which sounds reasonably close to a definition of policy development.

A little more than a decade later Frank Goodnow wrote his famous book on the theme of *Politics and Administration*. [12] The early civil service acts and the development of the civil service idea over many decades depended upon and contributed to the notion that politics and policy were, or should be, separated from administration. Parenthetically, the field of public administration as a legitimate area for academic study in its origins and development depended heavily upon the dichotomy; most students in this field for many years hung their hats on he rack of efficiency and disclaimed involvement in policy matters. Some still do.

Consistent with the ideal of political neutrality, the civil service reformers sought an organizational device which would immunize appointments and in-service activity from political influence. The civil service agency must be above and outside of the political arena—i.e. to a considerable degree independent of Congress and the Executive. To ensure its own integrity, it should be a multi-membered body, preferably representing both political parties so that no single leader might undermine its political neutrality. In consequence of this reasoning the civil service commission was invented. It was to become the basic model for personnel organization in the states and cities across the land, as well as a model of organization for the independent regulatory commissions which followed it. In keeping with Constitutional strictures as to the President's powers of appointment, the framers of the Pendleton Act provided that the Commissioners be appointed by the President with Senatorial approval, and were careful not to empower the Commission to make appointments to federal offices itself. Instead, it was to provide lists of the three best qualified applicants for a job from which the appointing officer might choose. And so was born the "rule of three."

Although the Congressional debates which preceded pass-

12. F. J. Goodnow, *Politics and Administration* (New York, The Macmillan Company, 1900).

age of the Pendleton Act showed that some of its proponents viewed the Civil Service Commission as a staff aid to the President, in practice it assumed a much more independent posture. It became an offsetting power unto itself against political pressures from the parties, the Congress, the President, and other units in the administration. It became not alone an instrument for the orderly administration of a merit system, but a watchdog against possible transgressions against such a system. In most of the states and local governments which imitated the federal civil service system, the independence and autonomy of the commissions were given an even more solid legal base. Viewed in historical perspective, the existence and the operations of the civil service commissions at all levels had two lasting effects. First, they perpetuated the association of public personnel and its administration with morality, the theme of the nineteenth-century reformers. Second, to a greater or less extent they divorced personnel administration from general management—from the executives responsible for carrying on the programs and activities of governments.

IV. 1906-37: GOVERNMENT BY THE EFFICIENT

Civil service reform accepted without much question the Jacksonian doctrine of simplicity. In the early years its principal, indeed almost exclusive, targets were jobs at the clerical level, and examinations were fairly elementary achievement tests. Yet, the civil service system provided a compatible base for the development during the first third of this century of technology and specialization. Its emphasis upon objectivity, upon relating qualifications with job requirements, and upon eliminating as far as possible considerations of personality and individual belief from personnel decisions were perfectly consistent with the ethos of scientific management. Further, the organizational separation and semi-independence of civil service administration provided encouragement to the development of scientific techniques in the personnel field itself. And the doctrine of separation of policy from administration, which lent support to the ideal of a politically neutral civil service, could equally rationalize the development of a highly specialized, technically competent administration.

The development of the field (or the science, or the discipline) of public administration during the first third of this century may be regarded either as an offshoot of scientific management in the public sphere or as an essentially parallel and similar movement. In much of their philosophy, approach, and content, the two were very nearly identical.[13] Both were grounded in a society thoroughly dedicated to growth and progress; in a philosophy of rationality; and in a faith in science and scientific method and its applicability to the practical lives of men and women, a reawakening of August Comte's positivism. Both proclaimed a new gospel to a new deity: efficiency. The precise meaning of the term was —and today remains—arguable, but its moral significance could hardly be questioned. Efficient administration was "good"; inefficient administration was "bad." It may be noted that the new "good" of efficiency did not, so far as the public service was concerned, displace the older one of a politically neutral merit system. The two deities complemented and supported each other. We had a diarchy, comparable to that of William and Mary in seventeenth-century Britain. The public service, to be good, must be both politically neutral and efficient, and there was more than a little doubt that it could be efficient unless it was also politically neutral.

Scientific management had begun in the latter part of the nineteenth century as a bundle of techniques—loosely woven into a "philosophy"—to make industry more efficient. Later, it broadened its scope to encompass other sectors of

13. As Waldo has demonstrated in *The Administrative State*, Chapter 3.

private business and eventually parts of government. The parallel movement in public administration, starting a bit later, was seen, in part at least, as an effort to make government more business-like, meaning, literally, more like business. The forms, structures, and procedures useful in business could be equally beneficial in government. Unlike administrative reform movements in most countries of the world, the American efficiency movement began and gained its momentum at the local rather than the national level. Its first targets were the cities, no doubt because they were the seat of most of our governmental scandals. But there were other contributing factors. One was that most American government was, at the turn of the century, local. In 1902, nearly three-fifths of all direct public expenditures were made at the local level; and if spending related to national defense is excluded, the local portion was nearly three-fourths. Another was that a large portion of what cities did was relatively routine, physical, and visible: maintaining and cleaning streets, water supply, refuse disposal, fire protection, etc. The principles and methods proved in business seemed readily applicable to such activities.

Public and private scientific management utilized many of the same tools and approached the subjects with similar concepts. These included:

1. *rationality:* the applicability of the rule of reason, based upon research, to the organization, management, and activities of men;
2. *planning:* the forward projection of needs and objectives as a basis for work programs;
3. *specialization:* of materials, tools and machines, products, workers, and organizations;
4. *quantitative measurement:* applied as far as possible to all elements of operations, including the qualifications of individuals to do specific jobs;
5. *"one best way":* there is one single best method of doing a job, and also one best tool, one best material, *one best type of worker;*

6. *standards and standardization:* the "one best," once discovered through systematic research, must be made the standard and thereafter systematically followed.

All of these added up to "efficiency," meaning roughly the maximization of output for a given input, or the minimization of costs for a given output (which is sometimes called economy).

In its application to governmental personnel, scientific management greatly added to the substance of civil service administration. Jobs could now be studied in terms of the duties involved and the qualifications necessary to execute them; they could be scientifically differentiated one from the other and standardized into classes having similar requirements. This will be recognized as the basis for *position classification. Examinations* could be framed to measure these qualifications scientifically, objectively, and competitively. Merit acquired a substance beyond honesty, basic education, general intelligence, and political neutrality. Thanks in part to the aptitude testing of the Army in World War I, personnel testing by civil service organizations became perhaps the most nearly "scientific" of all activities in the personnel realm. *Training* became an approved personnel function as long as it was restricted to the provision of knowledge and skills necessary to specific classes of positions, a restriction which is still applied in the majority of American jurisdictions. A new near-science of *efficiency ratings* was developed to provide a more objective basis for supervision and (often in conjunction with competitive examinations) as a determining force in promotions. By 1930, these activities had become the core of public personnel administration in the civil service. Among them the central hub was position classification because, according to the concept of scientific management, the content and the requirements of the position— or class of comparable positions—controlled all the other elements in the process. Personnel administration was effectively depersonalized.

I have so far emphasized the likenesses, indeed the identity, of scientific management in the private realm and public administration in the first third of this century. But there were profound differences arising from the contexts in which the two movements grew and lived, differences of basic significance to our present understanding of democracy and the public service. Some of these arose from the nature of the auspices and leadership of the two movements. Frederick W. Taylor, the inventor of scientific management, grew up through experience as apprentice, foreman, manager, and finally consultant for manufacturing concerns. The outlet and forum for his thoughts was initially the American Society of Mechanical Engineers. His colleagues and disciples were principally engineers and economists, both searching for rationality in decision-making in private business. There was an underlying faith that what is good in private business (i.e. efficiency) is good for the society as a whole. But the main point here is that the stimulus and the control of management were internal; there was no suggestion in the scientific management movement that outsiders have a role in advising or directing what is "good" except through the mechanisim of the market. Companies could hire good (meaning efficient) managers or they could engage private management consulting firms. But this was their option.

The development of scientific management in the governmental sphere was sparked and for several decades was powered by bureaus of municipal research, institutions unique to the public domain in this country and apparently indigenous to the United States. Beginning with the New York Bureau of Municipal Research, which was established in 1906, public administration assumed a quite different posture in its relation to its subject matter. The bureaus were not generated or supported *within* the public organizations they undertook to advise, nor did they sell their wisdom and services to those organizations for profit. Most of the early bureaus were privately sponsored and financed, usually by philanthropic agencies or individual philanthropists, and they derived much of their strength and influence from the very fact that they were *outside* and therefore presumably independent of government. They proceeded on the premise that the citizenry had a right, even an obligation, to know what the government was doing and how it was doing it. They could be, and often were, publicly critical of the ways in which governments conducted their business. The bureau movement from its origin invoked a sense of citizen responsibility, right, and participation entirely foreign to the scientific management movement in private business. In the process, it attracted and recruited leaders of a quite different type. The early leaders in public administration sought efficiency, but they were also deeply committed to political democracy as they saw it. One need only read the writings of many of them—such as Bruère, Cleveland, Gulick, Beard, and Mosher—to recognize the duality of their drive toward efficiency and democracy and their efforts to reconcile the two. Though some were trained in engineering and some in economics (and some of course in other fields) , the underlying discipline most congenial to their views was a heavily value-laden political science.

The disciples of scientific management in government had another difficulty to surmount: the matter of objectives. Taylor and his disciples had stressed that their system would result in greater benefits and wages to the workers, as well as to owners and investors, and later that it should benefit society in general. Its fundamental purpose from the start, however, was increased returns in relation to resources applied and this could be measured in terms of money—a criterion which was at once specific, quantifiable, and demonstrable. No such simple objective applied in most of the public sector. In the traditional lexicon of the economists, there was no market, no supply-demand relationship to determine prices, no "invisible hand" to rule out the inefficient. In the early days of the public administration movement, this problem was alleviated by the fact that most of the objectives of city governments were *givens;* products could be measured and evaluated against established purposes. Objectives were established by constitution, law, and ordinance. The job of administration was simply the carrying out, in the most efficient (or least expensive) manner, of objectives determined elsewhere. Thus was strengthened the distinction between policy and administration which had earlier supported the concept of the neutral civil service. Policy (i.e. objective) should be determined by representatives of the people—the legislature and the chief executive; execution should be effected by efficient and neutral administrators. Perhaps the most explicit and erudite statement of this view was made by Herbert A. Simon in his first book, *Administrative Behavior,*[14] in which he stressed the distinction of logical positivism between values (the sources of policy, which should be legislative) and facts (the basis of efficiency and the province of administration). As the bureau movement grew out of its city shell and became the nucleus of a general public management movement, the handling of the objectives problem became increasingly difficult. For many of the objectives of governments other than cities were social, not readily measurable, and difficult for legislature or executive to define with any degree of exactitude. This was particularly true of new programs, such as those undertaken during the New Deal and, more recently, the Great Society.

The policy-administration rationale was further challenged during this period by the growth in size and specialization of the public service itself. At the same time, civil service coverage and protection were penetrating higher and higher in governmental hierarchies. Such extension was, however sporadic, usually occurring in the later years of a president's term. Often too it was set back temporarily after a president of a different party took office. Increasing num-

14. New York, The Macmillan Company, 1947.

bers of highly specialized and professional jobs as well as positions of great administrative responsibility became part of the so-called classified civil service.[15] The extension of civil service coverage "upward, outward, and downward" [16] was a central theme of most governmental reformers during this period at every level of government. The campaign was not without success. By 1930, civil service protection extended to four-fifths of the non-military federal service and, following a slump during the early New Deal years, climbed again to about the same percentage level after 1940. This compares with 10 per cent in 1884.

The technical and specialized development of much of the public service, coupled with the extension of civil service protection to the great majority of employees, put an increasingly severe ideological strain on the doctrine of separation of politics and policy from administration. Growing numbers of positions at and near the top of administrative organizations were filled by career civil servants who obviously could influence if not control policy matters, matters which the "pure" literature proclaimed should be governed by politically responsible officials. Further, as bureaus were increasingly staffed by highly specialized career personnel, it became more and more difficult for non-expert political superiors and legislators to control their activities effectively. The relationship of policy and politics to administration had been a minor theme in American administrative and political theory until about 1900, and for a good many decades it had not been sounded at all. After that, however, and particularly up to the beginning of World War II it was in crescendo and came to be the number one issue for many students of American government. Indeed between the two world wars there was hardly a single important scholar interested in

15. The word "classified" has a somewhat special connotation in this federal usage, denoting coverage under the Civil Service law, not position classification.
16. The words used by President Roosevelt's Committee on Administrative Management in 1937 in its recommendation for civil service growth.

public administration who failed to pronounce his views on
the subject.[17]

One of the more extreme extensions of the politics-ad-
ministration dichotomy appeared in the view that *all* of
administration is, or should be, politically neutral and divorced from policy determination. It followed that all the
top-level administrative positions should be filled by merit
and protected in their tenure. It was but a short step from
this argument to the proposal of an administrative class, comparable in some respects to that of the British. The concept
behind the city manager movement was not far different
from this view: the council would be political in the policy
sense (though preferably non-partisan); the manager would
be a trained administrator, the servant of the council to carry
out its judgments, but otherwise divorced from policy. And
though he would not be protected by civil service, he would
nonetheless be appointed on the basis of merit as administrator. The city managers and their organization, the International City Managers' Association, have long since moved
away from this extreme position with regard to their proper
relation to policy, but they remain almost the only generalist public administrative class in the nation. Comparable
proposals were made to establish appointive state managers
on the basis of administrative merit, replacing or supple-
menting the elective governors.[18] Civil service selective procedures and protection were extended to an increasing number of bureau chiefs in Washington, and some advocated
inclusion of all of them. In some cities and states competitive
written examinations governed the choice of high officials up
to and including heads of departments, who also received
civil service protection.

Like other public activities during the efficiency period,

17. See Waldo's Chapter 7, "The Separation of Powers," op. cit., for an
interesting review and analysis of the many variations on this theme, especially
during the twenties and thirties.

18. For example, see Harvey Walker, *Public Administration in the United
States* (New York, Rinehart and Co., 1937), p. 81.

the public personnel function developed and applied objective and, hopefully, scientific techniques. Also like other specialized groups, the personnelists sought separatism and autonomy in the pursuit of their discipline, protected from politicians, administrators, employees, or interest groups who might threaten professional standards. The lay civil service commission, clothed by law with power over personnel activities and endowed with a substantial degree of autonomy, provided an admirable device for insuring such protection. The commission, invented by the reformers in the nineteenth century in quite a different setting and for quite different reasons, provided an effective canopy for the fostering of the personnel specialisms, one which gave other professional groups in government cause for imitation.

V. 1937–55: GOVERNMENT BY ADMINISTRATORS

The shift in ideological emphasis from efficiency, à la Taylor, to management, à la Brownlow, grew from seeds planted well before 1937. And management never replaced efficiency as a goal; it complemented and competed with it. Its biggest impetus was probably the Great Depression of the thirties when it became clear that government must assume a positive role in dealing with the problems of the society and the economy. Theretofore, most of government's activities—and most thinking about its role—concerned the provision of pretty well established services. With the New Deal, government ceased to be merely a routine servant or a passive and reactive agent. It became itself an initiator of programs and change—for a while, almost the only one. This role was strengthened during World War II when government, military and civil, dominated much of American life.

In this context, more important than efficiency in carrying out given tasks were initiative, imagination, and energy in the pursuit of public purposes. Those purposes were political, and the administrators charged with responsibility for them, as well as many of their subordinates, had to be politically sensitive and knowledgeable. Herein lay a new dimension in thinking about the public service which neither the early reformers nor the disciples of scientific management had contemplated.

Convenient bench marks of this period were the studies and reports of President Roosevelt's Committee on Administrative Management (the Brownlow Committee, which reported in 1937) and President Eisenhower's Commission on Organization of the Executive Branch of the Government (the second Hoover Commission, which reported in 1955). A central theme of the Brownlow Committee—perhaps *the* central theme—was the centeralization of power and responsibility in the President. His *executive* power was read to include *administrative* power; and administrative power was read to include both the execution of established policies and the initiative in developing new ones. In order effectively to exercise these powers certain fundamental changes were necessary, and these now read almost as the traditional *commandments* of public (and private) administration:

there should be clean, uninterrupted lines of direction from top to bottom, and of responsibility from bottom to top;

the President's span of control should be reduced to a manageable number by the consolidation of all administrative agencies into a limited number of departments;

independent agencies (principally the regulatory commissions) should be brought within the framework of appropriate departments for all purposes except those purely judicial in nature;

the President's competence with respect to his administrative responsibilities should be greatly strengthened ("The President needs help.") by providing him an immediate White House Staff with a "passion for anonymity"; and by giving him complete authority over the key staff functions of fiscal management, personnel, and planning.

At the time, there was vigorous dissent against the "dictator" bill by legislators, the press, and a good many scholars led principally by the Brookings Institution, which denied the basic premise that the executive power encompassed the administrative power. Over the years, however, the main ideas became standard among most administrative reformers and students of government. A good many found their way into governmental practice, and the central theses were implicit in the reports of both Hoover commissions, in later studies in the states by "little Hoover commissions," and in local-government reform movements.

Although the Brownlow Committee did not explore the point, the plain implication of its proposals was emphasis upon generalist administrative qualifications for those holding intermediate positions in the hierarchy. The Civil Service Commission had only recently broken the dike by providing for the recruitment and examination of college graduates on the basis of their general knowledge and intelligence for unspecified positions which were presumed to lead to administrative leadership opportunities. The National Institute of Public Affairs was recruiting interns from the colleges, and graduate training in public administration was accelerating on many campuses. There was widespread feeling against the narrowly conceived specialist and technician in administrative positions. Public administrators might or might not be trainable in administrative subject matter—the point was debated—but in any case they should be broadly educated, energetic men and women, developed through experience and protected by a merit system.

Although the management movement favored the extension of civil service coverage to the vast majority of civil positions in government, its main thrust was unfriendly to many aspects of the civil service tradition as it had developed over the years. In this respect its intent was quite opposite to that of the earlier efficiency movement. "Personnel" administra-

tion superseded "civil service" administration. Personnel was
seen as a principal, if not the major, tool of managemen As
such its administration should be organized as a staff aid
integral to the operating organization, not as a semi-independent agency. It should be headed by a single officer, appointed and removable by the executive, rather than by a
collegial commission. It should operate primarily as a service
to managers up and down the line, not as a watchdog and
controller over management. At the top level—i.e. at the
level of the chief executive—it should be concerned with the
development of standards and policies. Personnel operations,
on the other hand, should be decentralized and delegated to
bring them into more immediate relationship with the middle and lower managers whom they served. Personal and interpersonal considerations should be reintroduced into
personnel administration, even if they cost some degree of
objectivity and of scientific technique.

Variations on these themes found their way into many of
the studies and reports during this period at all levels of
government, and over the years had tremendous impact
upon the role of personnel administration in the total governmental process. The commission form of organization,
however, proved its resilience to such attack and still prevails
in most American jurisdictions which have a formal civil
service (or personnel) system.

The Brownlow Committee itself seemed little troubled
by the policy-politics and administration dichotomy. It held
simply that: "The preservation of the principle of the full
accountability of the Executive to Congress is an essential
part of our republican system," and sought to make such
accountability more effective, especially on the fiscal side.
Within the Executive, it sought to push the merit system upward to include "all permanent positions in the Government
service except a very small number of a high executive and
policy forming character. . . . The positions which are actually policy-determining, however, are relatively few in

number. They consist, in the main, of the heads of executive departments, under secretaries and assistant secretaries, the members of the regulatory commissions, the heads of a few of the large bureaus engaged in activities with important policy implications, the chief diplomatic posts, . . ." A line between policy-politics and administration could and should be maintained, not as between the executive branch and the legislature (though this position was still held at the municipal level by some city manager advocates) but as between a handful of political appointees at the top of federal agencies and their subordinates, all of whom should be in the civil service system.

This was a convenient rationale (or rationalization), and it was protected for the next fifteen years by there being no change in party control of the Presidency. But it was less than satisfying to the academic community, who were even then beginning to consider policy-making, if not politics, as an integral part of administration and were working this concept into their administration curricula. Obviously, during the New Deal period and the war which followed it most new policies and programs were initiated in the executive branch, often, if not usually, well below the levels of political appointees; obviously too, the Congressional committees were heavily involved in administrative detail. In the field of government, as well as in most social sciences, academic understanding, writing, and teaching seem to lag behind the world of reality. Most teachers and scholars (and many others who would become teachers and scholars) were drawn into government service during the New Deal and the war years, and they observed and participated in the initiating or making of policy up and down the administrative lines; they also observed the interest of Congress in the details of administration. A few might dismiss the incongruence of what they saw with what they had taught or been taught on the ground of emergency conditions, or on the ground that it was "bad" government which should be corrected as soon as possible after "that man" in the White House was replaced. Even these must have been disturbed later when, even after the war and after Roosevelt, policy-politics and administration refused to sort themselves out.

Soon after the end of the war there began to appear a new literature which directly or indirectly, explicitly or implicitly, attacked the old dichotomy. Paul H. Appleby insisted that administration itself is essentially a political process—and perhaps the most important one.[19] Harold Stein directed a series of case studies whose objectives included the provision of realistic insight into the interlocking of policy and administration; the first published collection of the cases was in fact entitled *Public Administration and Policy Development*.[20] In 1954 Norton E. Long pronounced that "However attractive an administration receiving its values from political policy-makers may be, it has one fatal flaw. It does not accord with the facts of administrative life." [21]

But not all students, or public officials, or citizens, accepted the demise of the policy-administration dichotomy, nor have they today. As already noted, Herbert A. Simon gave it new life in the academic community by identifying it, more or less, with another asserted separation between values and facts; and his view over the years has influenced and motivated substantial numbers of younger social scientists toward a "true science" of administrative decision-making based upon objective facts and rational analysis, with value-objectives to come from elsewhere—that is, from the people through their elected representatives. The First Hoover Commission in large part accepted and built upon the premises of the Brownlow Committee, concentrating on the orderliness and efficiency with which policies could be carried out. But the issues, which had long festered as an essentially intellectual (though nonethe-

19. In virtually all of his books, including especially that entitled *Policy and Administration* (University, Alabama, University of Alabama Press, 1949).

20. New York, Harcourt, Brace and Company, 1952.

21. In "Public Policy and Administration: The Goals of Rationality and Responsibility," *Public Administration Review*, XIV, 1 (1954), p. 23.

less important) problem, became a thumping reality with the election of President Eisenhower in 1952. The return of the Republicans to executive power after twenty years in the wilderness laid bare with shocking impact the problems of political transition: essentially, how to make a public service, in theory largely civil service protected and politically neutral, responsive to new political leadership. The situation was aggravated by many factors:

over the two preceding decades, the size of the federal service had multiplied several times, and its importance in the society and its diversity and complexity had grown even more;

few Republican leaders with any federal experience were availble and many of those who had worked with the Democrats were suspect in the new administration;

the great majority of the existing public servants were protected under the Civil Service law, and a great many of them had been blanketed in, instead of entering through the approved competitive route;

the public service had been itself a target of Republican political attack duing the 1952 campaign, and this attack, led by Senator McCarthy, was in fact to become more virulent during the early years of Republican leadership;

the new President, committed to a policy of retrenchment, could in only a very few cases satisfy partisan demands for jobs and power through new agencies and programs.

Among the consequences of this contretemps was a considerable degree of mutual suspicion between the incoming political appointees and the career officers whose activities they were presumed to oversee and, in a few agencies, a breakdown in communications between them. Many of the newcomers doubted that the incumbents would change their behavior in accordance with the objectives of the new administration—or could do so even if they wanted to. Some feared, and may even have experienced, sabotage in the carrying out of changed policies. In all of this was a recognition that some protected civil servants were in positions which could influence effective public policy, even though its pronunciation might come from above and from the Congress. Had the merit system been carried too far?

The new administration thought it had. Three months after his inauguration, President Eisenhower established a new exempted Schedule C to house a number of positions of a "policy-determining" or "confidential" nature which had previously been in the competitive service. In July 1953 a second Hoover Commission was established with broadened jurisdiction to consider not alone the efficiency of internal administration, like its predecessor, but also public policies. One of its principal foci, and probably its most significant contribution, was its study of the personnel system. Its report on "Personnel and the Civil Service" and the accompanying task force report were the first intensive treatments of the political executives, the career executives, and the relationships between the two. It was also the first major study to recommend that the number of political appointees at the top not be contracted—a reversal of a seventy-year trend. The central theme, however, did not change: [22]

"In the 160-odd years since a two major-party system developed in the United States, the American people have sought to achieve a workable balance between two vital requirements in the management of their Federal civilian employees. One requirement, arising out of the periodic rotation of the political parties in power, is that the officials responsible for establishing and defending Government policies and programs, the noncareer executives, should be selected by the successful party. This is vital if the party is to be really accountable to the people and if it is to carry out effectively the mandates and promises upon which it is elected. The other requirement is that there must be numerous trained, skilled and nonpartisan employees in the Federal service to provide continuity in the administration of the Government's activities."

22. Commission on Organization of the Executive Branch of the Government, *Personnel and Civil Service* (February 1955), p. 1.

The commission, unlike its predecessors, undertook to spell out with precision the proper bases of distinction between executive offices which should be politically filled and those which should be filled on a career basis within the civil service system. The former should include all positions which are filled by presidential appointment; exercise statutory or delegated authority to make final decisions as to "governing policies, programs, objectives"; and require public advocacy in justifying or defending governing policies. In addition, the commission recognized as warranting political appointments those non-executive positions "of a personal and confidential nature." The commission's Task Force estimated a maximum of about 800 positions which should properly qualify for political executive status. Career administrators, on the other hand, should be relieved of responsibilities for public advocacy or defense of policies and "should be kept out of direct participation in political controversies." The best of these at the top should be carefully selected and made part of a special group to be known as the Senior Civil Service, comprising ultimately about 3000 positions. These should be administered separately and according to quite different principles from the rest of the civil service. They should be transferable from one position to another without regard to the classification of their positions—i.e. rank was to reside in the man rather than in the job. They would have an obligation to serve "where needed most." They should be politically neutral.

This proposal of the Second Hoover Commission had little immediate impact on the "real" world,[23] yet it was perhaps the conceptual acme of the period I have labeled Government by Administrators (who were then and henceforth labeled executives). Its heavy emphasis upon the top groups, as distinguished from the rest of the public service, gave impetus to

23. The Senior Civil Service proposal sputtered and fizzled in the late fifties; the demarcation between political and career offices and officers seems no sharper and clearer today than in 1953; and career servants continue to be active and public advocates on policy issues.

an unprecedented interest in this area which was reflected in research, writing, and action programs during the decade that followed. Its implicit concept that there are identifiable, learnable principles and skills in administration as such— that an administrator can transfer from one kind of executive post to another without loss in effectiveness—capped a line of reasoning which had been developing for several decades.

The commission breathed new life into the distinction be-tween policy-politics and administration. Like the Brownlow Committee it drew the line not between legislature and ad-ministration, as the early doctrine, epitomized in the city manager plan, had done; and not among the legislative power, executive power, and administration, as the Brookings Institution had advocated. It sought to draw the line within the executive branch itself between those who were politically appointed and removable and those who were in the career civil service. Prominent among its critics, predictably, were students who had already voiced their doubts that the dichot-omy was or could be realistic.[24] Some feared that the senior civil service would become a built-in, protected governing elite—an administrative class (as in Great Britain) camou-flaged in the garb of political innocence and policy neutrality. They felt that the establishment of such an elite was contrary to and would threaten the underlying principles of American democracy.

It cannot be said that the commission's critics came up with any very satisfactory theory to substitute for the policy-politics and administration division, but a variety of alternatives were proposed. One recognized a third category of appointive of-ficers lying between the political appointees whose party iden-tification is a reason and condition of appointment and the career appointees who hold permanent tenure: individuals appointed because of their competence in a given field and because they are sympathetic with the objectives of the cur-

24. E.g. Paul H. Appleby, Stephen K. Bailey, Harlan Cleveland, Wallace S. Sayre, and Herman Somers.

rent administration in that field. They are identified with and devoted to a particular direction in public policy.[25] They are not hired as career civil servants, for their main career may lie elsewhere than in government. But they are not politicians either, since they are employed with moderate to zero reference to party and they do not engage actively in politics. Some of them are what Richard Neustadt has more recently labeled "in-and-outers," available on a temporary basis as needed by an administration, regardless of its partisan identification.

This group of policy-program, non-political officers, a product of American pragmatism, developed into prominence in the New Deal and has continued to be important since. Some are appointed to political office outright. Some—a much greater number—are appointed to a career service. Some are appointed in some intermediate category as consultants, or dollar-a-year men, or reserve officers in the military or the foreign service. A great many of the third group—the "intermediates"—have found their way into a career-secured system. Collectively, they provide a highly significant bridge between politics and administration. But it cannot be said that they have yet been accommodated either in the theory or in the law of the public service.

A second alternative to the policy-administration dichotomy was found in the *pluralism* of interests and drives among and within administrative organizations, which in turn reflects the pluralism of interests and politics in the society at large. Public administrators are heavily engaged in policy and politics a good share of their time, but much of it is of a different order of politics from that represented by political parties, elections and votes in the Congress. It is controversy, competition, and negotiation among different factions within the bureaucracy itself. It consists in dealing with, responding to,

25. The existence and significance of this group has been recognized by a large number of students, including Paul H. Appleby, David Levitan, R. N. Spann, Herman Somers.

or resisting clienteles and other interest groups outside, and with Congressional groups and individual congressmen, themselves responsive to similar pressures. From this melee, it is maintained, will emerge a degree of order and balance roughly responsive to the people expressing themselves through organized groups.

Unadulterated pluralism, however, is no guarantor of the one-man, one-vote ideal of democracy, nor does it offer any assurance of creative development or progress. The interests of a great many people—notably minority groups and the poor —are hardly represented at all through indiscriminate and unguided pluralism. Among different agencies and programs there are vast inequalities in the outside support they can muster or the outside opposition they must resist. Further- more, unbridled pluralism has an inescapably centrifugal effect on the structure and fabric of government. Each agency which has effective interest group support from the outside seeks autonomy to operate in its own realm; if left alone the administration responding to this drive would become a congeries of fiefdoms, each going its own way alone and self- sufficient. The result would be a form of anarchy. Many of those who recognized reality in pluralism also recognized its limitations and dangers. The principal counteractive force against the latter they sought to find in the power of the exec- utive, himself elective and responsible to the whole people. They therefore strove to strengthen his position vis-à-vis the administration: through legal powers, a strong chain of com- mand, a limited span of control, a vigorous body of advisers and staff units directly answerable to him.

One may ask how we are to be assured that the President and his influential advisers and staff units—especially those which consist largely of career personnel—will behave responsibly for the good of the whole people. For the President, the nom- inating and electoral processes, the aspiration for an honor- able paragraph in history, the constraints of the next election may provide adequate safeguards. For the others, there is loyalty to his office and his person. There is also the somewhat hopeful concept that conscientious, educated, and well-disposed public servants will behave in the *public* (or general) *interest*. Though some latter-day critics have questioned the faith in, and the usefulness of, the public interest,[26] there can be no doubt that many of those who wrote about and reacted against the dangers of pluralism had faith in the public interest concept as offering a basis of viable goals. As Paul H. Appleby wrote concerning the review process of the Bureau of the Budget: [27]

"The budget is made not merely by technical processes; it is made in a field where mighty forces contend over it. It is not made in a public arena, but the public is somehow well represented. This is one of the most mystifying of governmental phenomena."

But heavy reliance upon the motivations of a relatively small group of anonymous men entails some confidence in their wisdom, in their humanistic upbringing and education, and in their morality. All of these became topics of great importance to those who rejected the notion that administration is or should be separate from policy, politics, and human values. Were not these high public officials a twentieth-century incarnation of Plato's philosopher-kings?

Whether pluralism, counteracted by the chief executive and a strengthened hierarchy, sprinkled with consideration of the public interest and a touch of Platonism, constitutes an adequate theory for public administration seems a bit doubtful. Still another ingredient—or perhaps the seed of a quite different theory—appeared during the period of Government by Administrators: *representative bureaucracy*. The expression was used—to my knowledge, for the first time—during World War II as the title of a book by J. Donald Kingsley [28] which addressed itself to the British administrative class.

---

26. See particularly Glendon R. Schubert in his book by that title.
27. In his article, "The Influence of the Political Order," *American Political Science Review*, XLIII, 2 (April 1948),p. 281.
28. Yellow Springs, Ohio, The Antioch Press, 1944.

Among his theses were: that the British civil service reforms of the nineteenth century were intended to transfer control of the government from the aristocracy to the new business bourgeoisie; that the administrative class continued to represent the latter and to strive for the perpetuation of its values; and that this situation was the source of many of Britain's governmental deficiencies during the war years. Kingsley, in his more general analysis, declared that

". . . the complexity of present-day government makes it nearly impossible either for Ministers or Parliament to exercise effective control over the Service without its consent, or even without its active assistance. In England today, the bureaucracy is responsible because it is concerned with being so; and that concern is a reflection of its representative character" (p. 274).

And later:

". . . the essence of bureaucratic responsibility in the modern State is to be sought, not in the presumed and largely fictitious impartiality of the officials, but in the strength of their commitment to the purposes that the State is undertaking to serve. . . . The view of the Civil Servant as a disinterested assembler of facts simply will not stand examination" (p. 274-5).

". . . bureaucracies are responsible only to the extent that they are *broadly* representative" (p. 279; italics mine).

"The influence of the bureaucracy is inescapably large in an industrial state. . . . [The British Civil Service] has been an appropriate and useful instrument of the ruling middle class and its power has been rooted in that fact—as have also its structure and ethos" (p. 281).

Kingsley's study with its faintly Marxian undertones elicited no comparable analysis in American government, perhaps because we had no such definable, homogeneous, and homogenized administrative class. He clearly merged the two meanings of representativeness described in Chapter 1: representativeness of origin and background and representativeness in serving the interests of segments of the population. Here too there was probably more justification for doing so in the conservative class structure of British society than in the United States. Reinhard Bendix's 1949 study of *Higher Civil Servants in American Society* [29] revealed a quite remarkable degree of heterogeneity in the social backgrounds of federal bureaucracy, in striking contrast with the British and with the Federalist period in our own history. He concluded that ". . . in the American setting such background factors as social origin, education, and previous career-lines fail to show a homogeneity of administrators as a group that might conceivably militate against such impartiality." [30] Bendix posed no positive theory of bureaucratic representation as an element in democracy in the modern state, emphasizing only the absence of a cohesive administrative class which might threaten democracy.

But a vaguely defined idea of bureaucratic representation crept into, or was hinted at in, a number of studies and essays during this period. Perhaps its most explicit expression was given in a series of articles between 1949 and 1954 by Norton E. Long. Long deplored the weaknesses and the irresponsible behavior of elected and partisan legislatures, and viewed the administration as an antidote; a strong bureaucracy, far from being a threat to democracy, is its greatest pillar if it is sufficiently representative. Some of Long's points merit quotation: [31]

"Accustomed as we are to the identification of election with both representation and democracy, it seems strange at first to consider that the nonelected civil service may be both more representative of the country and more democratic in its composition than the Congress.

"As it operates in the civil service, the recruitment process brings into federal employment and positions of national power, persons whose previous affiliations, training, and background cause them to conceive of themselves as representing constitu-

29. Boulder, University of Colorado Press.
30. Ibid. p. 89.
31. All quotes are from Norton E. Long, *The Polity* (Chicago, Rand McNally & Company, 1962). The book is a collection of essays published over the previous twenty-five years.

encies that are relatively uninfluential in Congress. . . . the bureaucrats fill in the deficiencies of the process of representation in the legislature. . . .

"The democratic character of the civil service stems from its origin, income level, and association" (p. 70.).

". . . the bureaucracy now has a very real claim to be considered much more representative of the American people in its composition than the Congress" (pp. 71-2).

". . . the departments of administration come closer than any other organs of government to achieving responsible behavior by virtue of the breadth and depth of their consideration of the relevant facts and because of the representative character of their personnel" (p. 73).

But Long was no mere advocate of or apologist for powerful public administrators. He described representativeness in the administration as "seriously inadequate" (p. 72). In a later essay, he proposed that administration be deliberately structured so as to bring to bear on every policy problem proponents of differing points of view. He suggested building into the upper levels of the bureaucracy a "loyal opposition," comparable to that found in the legislature (p. 92). Recognizing and accepting the enormous power of the bureaucracy which derives from its command of facts, he proposed that it be staffed to give true expression to all major policy alternatives. This idea of building in potential opposition put him squarely at odds with the "administrative monotheism" of the First Hoover Commission—and indeed of the main thrust of the management movement as a whole.

It may be noted in passing that any theory of truly representative bureaucracy in a highly pluralistic society must also contemplate conflict within the administration as the milieu for decision-making. Administration would mirror all of the conflict and competition between and among the various interests and elements in the private sector. To a degree that might surprise a good many citizens, including political theorists, this has already developed in large sectors of our national administration, though not by conscious design. It is interesting that advocacy of representative bureaucracy, seen as a response to the dilemma posed by the collapse of the dichotomy of policy-politics and administration, should lead full circle to the argument that administration should be built upon internal conflict rather than a single, consistent, administrative hierarchy headed by the President.

Finally, it may be noted that representative bureaucracy, in theory at least, introduced a quite new dimension to personnel administration, at least for some positions. If individual officers are to be chosen to represent certain interests and points of view, clearly a merit system premised on efficiency and mastery of knowledges and skills appropriate to specific jobs is not adequate. In fact, it is pretty hard to accommodate the concept of representativeness within the bedrock core of classification and examinations. Furthermore, can one reasonably expect an appointee, recruited early with the expectation of spending most of his working life in the public service, to continue to represent and respond to outside interests and points of view for twenty or thirty or forty years? The idea suggests a drastic modification of the career concept itself to take care of "in-and-outers" so that fresh "representatives" may be injected continuously into the flow of public administrative decision-making.

RECAPITULATION

As the United States proceeded into the second half of the twentieth century, it bore a mixed and cumbersome baggage of concepts about the public service and about its role and control in a democratic polity. Each generation over its century and three-quarters history had contributed a wave of reform with features and emphases distinctive from any that had preceded. Each left lingering contributions and legacies even though some were subsequently modified. The more important of these are summarized below:

I. *Government by Gentlemen: 1789–1829*

      the standard of "fitness of character," appraised in terms of family background, educational attainment, high-ranking occupational experience

      high prestige of upper-level public service

      high moral standards of public office

      rotation in office of public executives following party change

II. *Government by the Common Man: 1829–83*

      the spoils system; appointments as a reward for party service

      equal opportunity for public office, subject to party loyalty

      the doctrine of simplicity of governmental work

      the sharp decline of public office and public service in popular and self esteem

      the legal profession as the source of most executive appointments

III. *Government by the Good: 1883–1906*

      civil service reform as a *moral* imperative

      the merit system linked primarily with competitive examinations

      an "open" service, with entry possible at all levels

      political neutrality of the civil service, and with it the separation of policy and politics from administration

      the civil service commission to govern administration of the service—a collegial, semi-independent, non-political, non-technical body

IV. *Government by the Efficient: 1906–37*

      efficiency as a second moral imperative

      a science of work and of management (including personnel management)

      position classification and the accompanying concept of rank and pay in the job rather than the man

      proliferation of specializations, accompanied by the development of the career idea within each

V. *Government by Administrators: 1937–55*

      the emergence of *administrative management:* (1) as a researchable, teachable discipline; (2) as the unifying element in governmental leadership regardless of function and specialization managed; (3) as a legitimate professional career

centralization of power in the chief executive and from him down through a rationally organized hierarchy; staff and staff organizations (including personnel) as aids to general management

(consequently) the development of personnel administration under a single personnel director responsible to management and away from the semi-independent civil service commission

restatement of the dichotomy between policy-politics and administration, followed by a series of challenges to it

emergence of a new class of public servants, the "in-and-outers," who are policy oriented but non-political

pluralism within public administration, reflective of that outside

representative bureaucracy

In terms of current American concepts about the public service, the sequence of the ingredients suggested above is more significant than the fact that they were introduced. A good many similar notions have undoubtedly influenced the development of ideology about public service in most industrialized countries, but the sequence in most of them was different. Here the generally high character and caliber of the early administrations delayed the drive toward systematized merit systems. In the succeeding half-century the egalitarian philosophy—centered in populism and equality of opportunity—made great strides. By the time of the Pendleton Act a class-oriented, university-based civil service system was politically impossible. Hence ours was devised as an open system in which considerations of class or family or formal education were intentionally avoided. The corruption and scandal associated with the public service during the middle decades of the nineteenth century provided a moral groundwork for civil service reform, and this moral flavor persists today. The reform movement implicitly relied upon a separation of politics and policy from the work of administration. The separation was urgently advocated by some, resisted by others. The scientific management movement with its emphasis on efficiency re-enforced the separation. But the New Deal, the war, and the movement toward a *compleat* administrative management pretty well demolished it. They left no adequate substitute for a concept which though rational, logical, and convenient, was empirically indefensible.

4

The Professional State

It is not difficult, looking a good many years backward in time, to identify many of the main directions of significant periods, as I attempted to do in the preceding chapter. But hindsight comes a great deal easier than foresight. Every participant observer in our polity—and that includes just about all of us—is likely to have his own interpretation of what happened yesterday and what is happening today and his own prediction of what will happen tomorrow. The *reviewer* in the year 2000 will in all probability have much more perceptive understanding of our directions in the 1950's and 60's than do any of the *viewers* today. Yet I think it essential that we identify as best we can the main characteristics of our current situation and the large directions in which we are moving.

Different observers would of course pick out different trends. For example, many would emphasize that this is a period of ever-quickening *change,* that, unlike the past when government responded to change and at most sought only to modify or regulate it, today it is in fact a principal originator, designer, and engineer of change. The role of the public service is itself changing from the provision of recurring and routine services to the initiation and management of change.

Some would note that, since World War II, our polity and our economy have been heavily, perhaps dominantly, influenced by *war* and the threat of war. A great part of the changes going on in our society are being fueled by the need for improvement in our state of readiness simply to keep up with our potential enemies, or keep a little ahead. Ours is a new kind of "garrison state" in which we are seemingly in a permanent condition of semi-mobilization and/or limited war. At the same time the technological, social, economic, and political spin-offs of this twilight condition may be more profoundly important than the immediate military situation and response.

Others would point to the current scientific revolution as the key distinguishing feature of our times, to the role of the public service in the development of science and, in turn, the impact of scientific developments upon the public service itself. This has been a theme of a number of books in recent years, including particularly that by Don K. Price, *The Scientific Estate*. Price identifies scientists as one of the four great estates in our society today, the others being the professions, administrators, and politicians. But Price's introductory and central thesis is that the scientific revolution ". . . seems certain to have a more radical effect on our political institutions than did the industrial revolution, for a good many reasons." Among these he notes three: (1) that it is "moving the public and private sectors closer together"; (2) that it is "bringing a new order of complexity into the administration of public affairs"; (3) that it is "upsetting our system of checks and balances." [1]

Still others would stress a new kind of *managerial revolution* which appears to be modifying the philosophy as well as the style of administration in both private industry and government. It is differently defined by different writers. Some emphasize the impact upon organizations of vast changes in information and communications systems brought about by computer technology and automation. Others, the significance of interpersonal relations, employee participation, and sensi-

1. Don K. Price, *The Scientific Estate* (Cambridge, Harvard University Press, 1965), pp. 15–16.

tivity—in contrast with the traditional views of organization
as a system of authority-responsibility relationships up and
down a hierarchy. Both of these are clearly having some fall-
out in the field of public personnel administration, including
the tendency to decentralize more of decision-making toward
the "line" managers and their subordinates, the growing
emphasis upon service rather than control in personnel operations, and a variety of devices to encourage employee participation.

Still others would choose to emphasize, particularly in the
years since 1960, the awakening of American society and the
response of its public service to the great domestic social problems, challenges, and responsibilities. Implicit in the slogans
of both President Kennedy and President Johnson, the New
Frontier and the Great Society, was the charge on all citizens
and particularly the public servants to improve the life of *all*
Americans—through stimulating economic growth, improving education, eradicating poverty, ending unemployment,
assuring equal rights and opportunities to minority groups,
eliminating segregation, lessening crime, improving housing,
solving the metropolitan problem, beautifying the countryside, and so on.

I would not criticize any of the above interpretations of the
current directions of our governments and public services. All
seem to me valid, and most will probably be considered to
have been important by the historians of the next generation.
But the characteristic of the public service—and indeed of a
great part of the rest of society—which seems to me most significant today is *professionalism*. If it is defined broadly, as it
is here, it relates to all of the types of emphasis suggested
above, and encompasses a substantial part of some of them.
Daniel Bell,[2] like Don K. Price before him,[3] recently wrote
of an emerging new society in which old values and social

2. "Notes on the Post-Industrial Society" I *The Public Interest,* 6 (Winter
1967), pp. 24–35.
3. Op. cit.

power associated with property, wealth, production, and industry are giving way to knowledge, education, and intellect.

"To speak rashly: if the dominant figures of the past hundred years have been the entrepreneur, the businessman, and the industrial executive, the 'new men' are the scientists, the mathematicians, the economists, and the engineers of the new computer technology. And the dominant institutions of the new society—in the sense that they will provide the most creative challenges and enlist the richest talents—will be the intellectual institutions. The leadership of the new society will rest, not with businessmen or corporations as we know them . . . , but with the research corporation, the industrial laboratories, the experimental stations, and the universities." [4]

If Bell and Price are near the mark, as I think they are, the importance of the professions, among which I would include the applied scientists in virtually all disciplines, is increasing rapidly and will continue to do so. Viewed broadly, the professions are social mechanisms whereby knowledge, including particularly new knowledge, is translated into action and service. They provide the means whereby intellectual achievement becomes operational.

The extent to which the professions have become dominant in American society has been noted by a number of commentators. In a recent issue of *Daedalus* which was entirely devoted to the professions, Kenneth S. Lynn maintained that: "Everywhere in American life, the professions are triumphant." [5] And Everett C. Hughes wrote in the same issue: "Professions are more numerous than ever before. Professional people are a larger proportion of the labor force. The professional attitude, or mood, is likewise more widespread; professional status more sought after." [6]

In statistical terms the U.S. Census reflects the accelerating

4. Bell, op. cit. p. 27.
5. *Daedalus,* Vol. 92, No. 4 (Fall 1963), p. 649.
6. Ibid. p. 655.

growth of what it terms "professional, technical, and kindred" workers, who grew from 4 to 11 per cent of the American labor force between 1920 and 1960. The fastest growth has been since World War II; it continues today and certainly will do so well into the future.

THE PROFESSIONAL PUBLIC SERVICES

The prominent role of American governments in the development and utilization of professions seems to have gone largely unnoticed. They are the principal employers of professionals. According to the 1960 Census, 36 per cent of all the "professional, technical, and kindred" workers in the United States were employed by governments, and this of course did not include a multitude of scientists, engineers and others indirectly employed through government contracts, subsidies, and grants. Looked at another way, about one-third of all government employees were engaged in professional and technical pursuits. This was more than three times the comparable proportion in the private sector. The governmental proportion is heavily inflated by school teachers, who are classified as professional. Even if they are omitted, however, the proportion of professionals in total public employment was nearly one-fifth, more than double the comparable proportion in the private sector.

Leaving aside the political appointees at or near the top of our public agencies and jurisdictions, the administrative leadership of government is increasingly professional in terms of educational and experiential backgrounds. This is not to say that public leadership as such is an administrative profession, rather that it consists of a very wide variety of professions and professionals in diverse fields, most of them related to the missions of the organizations in which they lead.

In government, the professions are the conveyor belts between knowledge and theory on one hand and public purpose on the other. The interdependencies between the professions and government are many. Governments are, or have been:

the creators of many professions

the legitimizers of all those which have been legitimized

protectors of the autonomy, integrity, monopoly, and standards of those which have such protections

the principal supporters of their research and of that of the sciences upon which they depend

subsidizers of much of their education

among their principal employers and the nearly exclusive employers of some of them, which means also

among the principal utilizers of their knowledge and skills

For their part, the professions:

contribute to government a very substantial proportion of public servants

provide most of the leadership in a considerable number of public agencies

through their educational programs, examinations, accreditation, and licensing, very largely determine what the content of each profession is in terms of knowledge, skills, and work

influence public policy and the definition of public purpose in those many fields within which they operate

in varying degree and in different ways provide or control the recruitment, selection, and other personnel actions for their members

shape the structure as well as the social organization of many public agencies

It may accurately be argued that there is nothing very new about professionalism in government. The principal spawning period for educational programs for the professions, as indicated in Chapter 2 above, was the first quarter of this century, and the U.S. Classification Act of 1923 established a professional and scientific service. In all probability the number of professionally educated personnel in all governments has been rising for the past half-century. Yet there appears to have been very little recognition of or concern about the significance of professionalism in the public service and its leadership until quite recently. For example, the Brownlow report and those of the two Hoover commissions, for all of their concern about administrative management, paid scant attention to professionals in fields other than management as such. Contrast the emphasis of recent studies. The Municipal Manpower Commission in its 1962 study of *Governmental Manpower for Tomorrow's Cities* [7] focused its entire report on what it called APT personnel, the abbreviations standing for administrative, professional and technical. Investigation of Federal personnel problems, such as that of the Herter Committee on Foreign Affairs Personnel [8] and the study of personnel problems of the Public Health Service, similarly have concentrated on professional and administrative positions. The same is true of various studies at the state and local levels, of which David T. Stanley's recent report on *Professional Personnel for the City of New York* [9] is a notable example. All of these inquiries have either taken for granted or have clearly indicated that a large part of the administrative leadership is now and will continue to be drawn from professional fields considered appropriate for the programs of particular agencies.

The degree to which individual professional specialisms have come to dominate public agencies is suggested by the small sample below. The right hand column indicates both the primary professional field in the agency and the normal professional source of its career leadership.

Federal

All the military agencies	Military officers
Department of State	Foreign Service officers
Public Health Service	Public health doctors
Forest Service	Foresters
Bureau of Reclamation	Civil engineers
Geological Survey	Geologists
Department of Justice	Lawyers
Office of Education	Educators
Bureau of Standards	Natural scientists

7. New York, McGraw-Hill Book Company.

8. *Personnel for the New Diplomacy* (New York, Carnegie Endowment for International Peace, December 1962).

9. Washington, D.C., The Brookings Institution, 1963.

State and Local

Highways and other public works agencies	Civil engineers
Welfare agencies	Social workers
Mental hygiene agencies	Psychiatrists
Public health agencies	Public health doctors
Elementary and secondary education offices and schools	Educators
Higher education institutions	Professors
Attorneys general, district attorneys, legal counsel	Lawyers

I define the word "profession" liberally as (1) a reasonably clear-cut occupational field, (2) which ordinarily requires higher education at least through the bachelor's level, and (3) which offers a lifetime career to its members.[10] The professions in government may conveniently be divided in two classes: first, those in fields employed in the public *and* the private sectors and for whom the government must compete in both recruitment and retention. This category, which I shall call "general professions," includes most of the callings commonly understood as professions: law, medicine, engineering, architecture, to illustrate. I also include among them applied scientists in general and college professors. Second are those employed predominantly and sometimes exclusively by governmental agencies, which I shall call "public service professions." Most of these were generated within government in response to the needs of public programs, and although there has been a tendency in the direction of increased private employment for many of them, governments are still the predominant employers. They fall in two classes: first, those which are employed exclusively by a single agency such as

10. The definition is unquestionably too loose to satisfy many students of occupations who would like to add other requisites, such as: professional organization; or eleemosynary or service orientation; or legal establishment; or individual autonomy in performance of work; or code of ethics. In terms of governmental consequences, the liberal usage is more appropriate. For example, in terms of their group behavior in government, the officers of the U.S. Navy are at least as "professionalized" as are lawyers.

military officers, Foreign Service officers, and Coast Guard officers; and second, those employed by a number of different governmental jurisdictions, such as school teachers, educational administrators, social workers, public health officers, foresters, agricultural scientists, and librarians.

Most of those listed above in both categories may be described as "established professions" in the sense that they are widely recognized *qua* professions and, with only a few exceptions, their status has been legitimized by formal state action through licensing, credentialing, commissioning, or recognizing educational accreditation.

In addition to these, there are many "emergent professions" which have not been so recognized and legitimized but which are valiantly and hopefully pulling themselves up by their vocational bootstraps to full professional status. In the "emergent" and "general" group are included, for example, specialists in personnel, public relations, computer technology, recreation, financial management, purchasing. "Emergent" in the "public service" category are governmental sub-divisions of all of these and some which are more exclusively governmental: assessors, police, penologists, employment security officers, air pollution specialists, etc.

The professions—whether general or public service, whether established or emergent—display some common characteristics which are significant for democracy and the public service. One of these is the continuing drive of each of them to elevate its stature and strengthen its public image as a profession. In a very few highly esteemed fields, such as law and medicine, the word "maintain" is perhaps more appropriate than "elevate." A prominent device for furthering this goal is the establishment of the clear and (where possible) expanding boundaries of work within which members of the profession have exclusive prerogatives to operate. Other means include the assurance and protection of career opportunities for professionals; the establishment and continuous elevation of standards of education and entrance into the profession; the upgrading of rewards (pay) for professionals; and the improvement of their prestige before their associates and, if possible, the public in general.

A second common denominator of the professions is their concentration upon the *work substance* of their field, both in preparatory education and in journeyman activities, and the differentiation of that field from other kinds of work (including other professions) and from work at a lower or subprofessional level in the same field. Accompanying this emphasis upon work substance has been a growing concentration, particularly in preprofessional education, upon the sciences which are considered foundational for the profession in question, whether they be natural or biological or social (behavioral). This emphasis is an inevitable consequence of the explosive developments of science in the last two decades, and unquestionably it has contributed to the betterment of professional performance.

Partially in consequence of the concentration upon science and work substance there has been a much less than parallel treatment of the *ecology* of the profession in the total social milieu: of the consequences and purposes of the profession and of the constraints within which it operates. There are signs in a good many fields today that attention to these topics is increasing, particularly in the public service professions. Yet much of professional education and practice is so focused on substance and science as to obscure the larger meaning of the profession in the society. Except for those professionals who grow beyond their field, the real world is seen as by a submariner through a periscope whose direction is fixed and immutable.

One of the most obscure sectors of the real world in professional education and much of its practice is the realm of government and politics. There is a built-in aversion between the professions and politics. Its origin is historical: most of the professions, and particularly those in the public service category, won their professional spurs over many arduous years to the extent they could escape the infiltration, the domination, and the influence of politicians (who, to most professionals, are by definition amateurs at best and corrupt ones at worst). Compare, for example, the evolution of the military, diplomatic, social welfare, city manager, and like fields. The aversion to politics has contemporary supports. Professionalism rests upon specialized knowledge, science, and rationality. There are *correct* ways of solving problems and doing things. Politics is seen as constituting negotiation, elections, votes, compromises—all carried on by subject-matter amateurs. Politics is to the professions as ambiguity to truth, expediency to rightness, heresy to true belief.

Government as a whole comes off not much better than politics in the eyes of most professions, particularly the "general" ones. In the first place, it carries the political taint by definition. Secondly, it violates or threatens some of the treasured attributes and myths of true professionalism: individual and professional autonomy and freedom from "bureaucratic" control; service to, and fees from, individual clients; vocational self-government. Among those general professions with large numbers of members employed privately, preservice education usually treats government (insofar as it is considered at all) as an outside agency with or against which one must deal. This seems to be true of most education in law, engineering, accounting, and some other business fields, upon all of which government is heavily dependent. It is also true of medicine and most of its sub-specialties. Even in many public service professions—public school education provides an excellent example—there is a considerable aversion to government *in general* and to politics—which may be another word for the same thing. Government is all right in those particular areas in which the specified profession has dominant control; but beyond those perimeters, it is equated with "politics" and "bureaucracy" in their more invidious senses.

I doubt that it is appropriate to speak of "strategies" of the professions in government because some of their consequences seem to have "just growed" rather than to have been consciously planned. Yet those consequences are fairly consistent, particularly among the established professions, whether of the public service or the general category. And the emergent professions are varying distances down the road. The pattern has these features:

(1) the given profession has staked its territory within the appropriate governmental agency or agencies, usually with boundaries coterminous with those of the organization itself;

(2) within its organization, it has formed an elite corps with substantial control over the operations of the agency, significant influence on agency policies, and high internal prestige;

(3) to the extent possible, it has assumed control over employment policies and individual personnel actions for its own members in the agency and also over the employment of employees not in the elite profession;

(4) it has provided its members the opportunities, assurances, and protections of a career system of employment.

The succeeding two sections will deal with items (2) and (3) above. The fourth, career systems, is treated in Chapter 5.

PROFESSIONAL ELITES

Our study and hence our understanding of public administrative organizations have for some time been conditioned by two primary considerations. One is simply the *past*, when most organizations were not professionalized and when it seemed logical to build on the premise that organization consisted of two essential elements: management and workers. The focus was upon the problems, the skills, the content of management viewed as a single, common task, regardless of the differing activities and objectives of the organizations.[11] The second source of our lore about public organizations de-

11. For examples see the works of Frederick Taylor, Henri Fayol, or Chester Barnard. Their main tenets were reinforced by the writings of Max Weber.

rives principally from studies of organizations in the realm of private business, but augmented by cases and analyses about some public or semi-public organizations usually at a fairly subordinate level of operations: military units, hospitals, mental institutions, prisons, schools, and scientific laboratories. The more recent organizational literature has recognized and even dwelt upon a third element of organization: the professionals, who are usually viewed as *staff*. They are organizationally below management but are often considered to be superior in educational and social terms.

So we begin our organizational analysis from a *trichotomy* which consists of management, workers, and professionals or staff. The professionals are analyzed in the degrees to which they are dedicated to their organizations, the "locals," or to their professions, the "cosmopolitans." There is a presumed conflict of interest between management and workers, between professionals and workers, and between management and professionals.

One hesitates to generalize as to the validity or usefulness of either the dichotomous or the trichotomous premises in non-public organization today. Undoubtedly they are still applicable in many industrial and commercial organizations. They seem quite inapplicable, however, in most of the professionalized agencies of government, and these include the most important ones. In these agencies:

the managers are professionals in the specialized occupational fields of their agencies—not as managers per se, for few have trained themselves for management;

most of those designated as staff are also professionals, but typically in fields of specialism different from the management;

many of the workers—and most of those in middle-management positions—are also professionals, usually in the same professions as management.

Commonly there is a mutually supportive relationship between the professional managers and the professional workers in the same profession. The former see themselves, and are viewed by the latter, as representative of the interests of both.

Further, there may be no conflict between the organization and its objectives on the one hand and the aspirations and standards of its professional workers and executives on the other. In a good many cases, the goals and standards of public agencies, as seen by their officers and employees, are identical with the goals and standards of the professions as they are seen by their members. This is true of most public organizations in fields such as health, welfare, geology, forestry, education, and military affairs. In other words the public organizations, the bureaucracies, not only heavily influence but actually determine and epitomize the goals of the professions which provide the leaders and many of the workers who work for them.

A more useful model of most sizable public organizations in government—at the department level and below in state and local units and at the bureau or service level and below in the federal government—would be one which recognized the internal professional and other vocational groupings and the stratification of these within each agency in terms of both prestige and power. In most public agencies which have been in operation for some time there is a single occupational group whose knowledge, skills, and orientations are closely identified with the mission and activities of the agency. If the work is seen as requiring intellectual capacity and background education to the level of college graduation—and as we have seen, this is the case in an increasing majority of agencies—the group comes to constitute a professional elite. It is a *corps*—a body of men and/or women closely associated with each other and with the enterprise—and it is sometimes so designated. It is also a *core*: it is at the center of the agency, controls the key line positions, and provides the main, perhaps the exclusive, source of its leadership. If at the time the elite developed there was no existing profession clearly identified with the activities of the agency, it is likely to be a unique

public service profession—military, Foreign Service, public
health, for example. If on the other hand there was a clearly
related existing outside profession or if one subsequently developed, the elite may consist of members of a *general profession*—as civil engineers in highway departments, psychiatrists
in mental hygiene institutions, and lawyers in departments of
justice. In some cases, the clearly different nature of the work
of the public agencies has occasioned a split-off from an established profession and the birth of a new public service profession, which, however, has retained the educational base of the
older one—as in the case of public health doctors and the
emerging professions of public works engineers and educational administrators.

There are five principal types of exceptions to the professional elite structure. One is found in new agencies such as the
Peace Corps or the Office of Economic Opportunity where no
existing profession can make a clear claim to status as the
appropriate elite. Here there is jockeying for position; but
one would guess that, within a decade, there would emerge
new public service professions. A second exception occurs in
agencies of the business type, such as the Post Office and some
publicly owned utilities, where the trichotomy of management, staff, and workers may be more accurate. (In many
utility operations, however, line management consists of professional engineers.) A third exception is found in those public agencies whose work does not (or does not yet) require
higher education to the graduating level. Police and fire protection are examples of this, though both are moving in the
direction of professionalization. Fourth are agencies which
are controversial, unstable or temporary, or which, for political reasons, must avoid the appearance of permanence. Professional elitism entails a career orientation. The Agency for
International Development is a good current example in
which the development of a technical assistance elite has been
politically inhibited. Finally, a few agencies were deliberately
designed in such a way as to prevent control by a single occu-

pation through their multi-purpose missions. An example is the Tennessee Valley Authority.

Professional elites in larger agencies tend to specialize into subdivisions under the general professional canopy. These may be reflections of well-recognized divisions of the profession, determined outside the agency and extending back into educational specialization, as in medicine and engineering. They may be grounded in specializations of work in the agency itself, sometimes highly formalized as in various arms and services of the Army (Engineer, Quartermaster, Infantry, Ordnance, etc.). Or they may be based upon continuing kinds of work assignments not formally recognized as separate corps —e.g. the distinctions among personnel officers in activities such as recruiting, examining, classification, labor relations. Among such sub-groups there is normally a pecking order of prestige and influence. The most elite of the sub-groups is likely to be the one which historically was most closely identified with the end purpose, the basic content of the agency— the officers of the line in the Navy, the pilots in the Air Force, the political officers in the Foreign Service, the civil engineers in a construction agency which also employs electrical and mechanical engineers, etc.

No organization of substantial size can consist solely of members of one profession. Always there must be supportive activities, carried on by individuals who are not members of the elite profession. Indeed, the number in the professional elite may constitute only a small minority of all employees; e.g. public health doctors in a local health office, psychiatrists in mental health institutions, social workers in welfare offices. Complex government agencies employ sizable numbers of professionals and specialists in fields other than the elite one. These may be grouped in the following main categories:

Supporting Line Professions whose members carry on and contribute to the substantive work of the agency, but are
trained and experienced in different fields. Thus in a
state mental health department and in state mental in-

stitutions the psychiatrists are the elite, but by far the greater numbers are psychologists, psychiatric nurses, and social workers. A forestry operation includes agronomists, botanists, engineers, and many others.

Staff Professions: advisers and technicians for their specialized knowledge in areas related to, but not central to, the line work of the agency—as economists, sociologists, legal counsel, design engineers, computer analysts, etc., in many kinds of agencies. These are usually few in number and relatively high in grade and position, though not at the very top.

Administrative Professions: officials engaged in personnel, budget, finance, communications, purchasing, supply, etc. Some of these can be found in almost every large agency, although in some the positions are filled by members of the elite professions, particularly at the level of leadership. Most of these are "emergent" rather than established professions.

Workers, including sub-professionals, supervisors, clerical, service, skilled, and unskilled personnel.

Chart I is a "still picture" of the composition of a hypothetical public agency, well-established and operating in a professional field.[12] The vertical dimension is organizational rank or level of pay, and may be assumed to equate very roughly with the level of day-to-day responsibility of incumbents. The horizontal dimension represents the numbers of persons at each grade. The horizontal lines at bottoms of the figures represent the normal and sometimes exclusive entering level of beginners when they are appointed in the various categories. The horizontal lines and points at the tops of the various figures represent the highest grade an individual in each category can expect to reach. For an employee to cross lines from one category to another is usually difficult and, where professional standards are high and clear-cut, may be impossible, even illegal. The diamond shapes of the elite

12. Hypothetical examples of the *schema* in particular kinds of agencies are shown in Chart II.

profession (2) and of the other professional groups (4 and 5) are typical of most such groups in government where professionals are hired soon after completing their education on a junior basis and advance rapidly to journeyman-level work. The trapezodial (as distinguished from the familiar pyramidal) shape of the organization as a whole is also representative, although in most agencies the percentage of the total who are professional personnel is much smaller than is represented on the chart. Over the course of time, the normal progress of an employee in any category is upward, but obviously only a few will make it all the way to the top.

At the top of the diagram are represented a small number of political appointees, recruited from outside, who may or may not be professional. With these are included some political appointees drawn from the elite segment of the elite profession. Most of the very top career jobs are also filled from this group, and almost all of such jobs are filled by the elite profession. The incumbents of these jobs constitute very roughly what Morris Janowitz described as the "elite nucleus." [13]

The diagram suggests that those who make it to the very top, the "elite of the elite," have pursued a more or less "orthodox" and "proper" type of career up the most favored ladder. The implication appears to be erroneous in some cases and may indeed be widely untrue. Janowitz found a substantial proportion of the military elite nucleus to be individuals who had pursued an unorthodox, innovative career. A recent study of the U.S. Foreign Service indicated that among the Foreign Service Officers (FSO's) in executive positions in Washington (Deputy Office Directors and above) and overseas (Chiefs of Mission, Deputy Chiefs, Consuls General) a disproportionate number had entered the service laterally (i.e. unorthodoxly). Between 1958 and 1962, both the number and proportion of orthodox, examination-entry officers in

13. In his study of *The Professional Soldier: A Social and Political Portrait* (Glencoe, Illinois, The Free Press, 1964), Chapter 8.

CHART I. SCHEMATIC DIAGRAM OF COMPOSITION OF A
PROFESSIONALIZED GOVERNMENT AGENCY

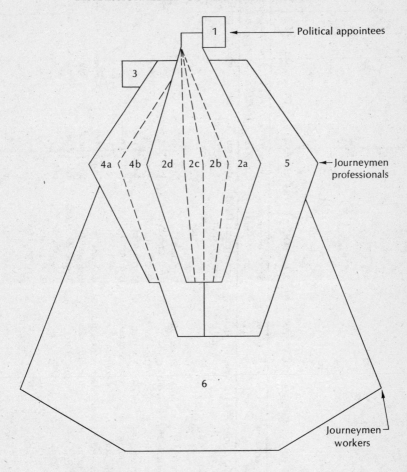

KEY: 1. Political appointees from outside the agency
2. The elite profession:
   2a. The elite segment of the elite profession
   2b, c, d. Other segments of the elite profession
3. Staff professions
4. Line professions
5. Administrative professions
6. Workers, including supervisors, sub-professionals, clerical, manual, and others.

CHART II. ILLUSTRATIVE BUT HYPOTHETICAL EXAMPLES OF SOCIAL ORGANIZATIONS OF PUBLIC AGENCIES

	Department of State	Department of Air Force	State Department of Highways	State Department of Mental Health	Local Department of Health
1. Political Appointees	Secy.; Under-secys. and some Asst. Secys.	Secretary, Under-secys. and Asst. Secys.	Department Head and Deputies	Department Head and Deputies	Department Head
2. Elite Profession 2a. Elite Segment 2b. Other " 2c. Other " 2d. Other "	FSO's Political Officers Economic " Consular " Administrative Officers	Air Force Officers Flying " Logistics " Maintenance " Administrative Officers	Engineers Civil Engineers Electrical " Mechanical " Industrial "	M.D.'s Psychiatrists Surgeons Gen. Practitioners Pathologists	M.D.'s Pub. Health M.D.'s Pediatricians Gen. Practitioners
3. Staff Professions	Legal Advisers Scientific Advisers Public Relations Officers Etc.	General Counsel Scientific Advisers Public Information Officers Etc.	Counsel Economists Public Relations Officers Real Estate Appraisers Etc.	Counsel Sociologists Statisticians Etc.	Counsel Sociologists Bio-statisticians Etc.

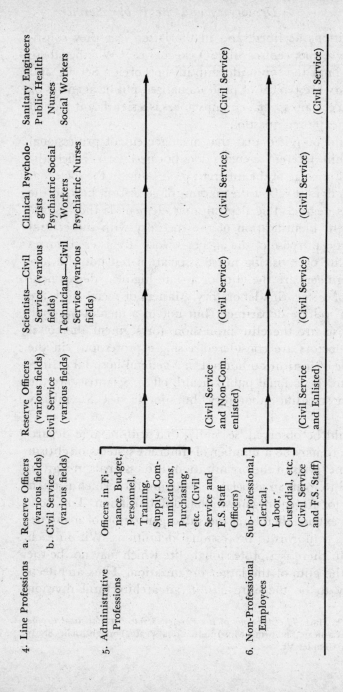

4. Line Professions

a. Reserve Officers (various fields)
b. Civil Service (various fields)

Reserve Officers (various fields)
Civil Service (various fields)

Scientists—Civil Service (various fields)
Technicians—Civil Service (various fields)

Clinical Psychologists
Psychiatric Social Workers
Psychiatric Nurses

Sanitary Engineers
Public Health Nurses
Social Workers

5. Administrative Professions

Officers in Finance, Budget, Personnel, Training, Supply, Communications, Purchasing, etc. (Civil Service and F.S. Staff Officers)

(Civil Service and Non-Com. enlisted)

(Civil Service)

(Civil Service)

(Civil Service)

6. Non-Professional Employees

Sub-Professional, Clerical, Labor, Custodial, etc. (Civil Service and F.S. Staff)

(Civil Service and Enlisted)

(Civil Service)

(Civil Service)

(Civil Service)

these positions declined, and in the latter year they constituted only 43 per cent of all FSO executives.[14] Whether these findings about the top leadership in the Foreign Service and the military are typical of professionalized public agencies or arise from certain special circumstances is a significant though largely unexplored question.

It should be noted that that arrangement of professional elites within different agencies does not necessarily reflect the status and prestige of the different professions in the society at large, nor does it reflect the amount of education beyond the bachelor's degree. The determining element is the historic and current identification of the specialty with the central content and purpose of the agency's work. Registered nurses are the elite of a visiting nurse association but not of a hospital. Engineers are the elite of a state highway department but not of a scientific laboratory. Masters of social work are elite in a welfare department but not in a mental hospital. Psychiatrists are the elite profession (or segment thereof if medical doctors are considered a single profession) in the latter type of institution but not in a general hospital or in a local, state, or national public health office. Scientists are the elite in a scientific laboratory, but not in a U.S. embassy overseas.

It should be observed, secondly, that within large departments there may be a number of different systems of elitism at different levels in the organization. Professionals in a given field tend to form an associational community which is often the basis for formal organizational differentiation. To a considerable extent, therefore, the sub-organization of many departments conforms to professional definitions. Within each major unit there is a professional elite which may not be the same as the elite of the larger organization. Thus architects are likely to be the elite *within* an architectural division

14. John E. Harr, *The Anatomy of the Foreign Service: A Statistical Profile* (New York, Carnegie Endowment for International Peace, Foreign Affairs Study No. 4, 1965), Chapter VI.

which includes many engineers among other professionals; but if the division is a part of a department of public works, the architects yield in elite status to the civil engineers at the departmental level. Similarly, psychiatrists are the elite segment in the National Institute of Mental Health but not in the U. S. Public Health Service as a whole.

Thirdly, it may be noted that the elite status of professions in many different public agencies is relatively but not completely stable. The knowledge, technique, and orientation of the older professions tend toward obsolescence in the face of growing science, new kinds of problems, and new understandings about how to deal with them. These tendencies cast the older professional elites in a stance which is at once defensive and conservative vis-à-vis their positions and their control over agency objectives and programs. The intra-agency structure of elitism is, in many organizations, a battle ground between a professional elite, or the elite segment thereof, and other professions, other segments, and non-professionals. Political leaders desirous of rapid development of new programs may, and frequently do, endeavor to tip the balance against the elite professionals by appointing or selecting for promotion individuals who represent points of view at variance with the elite—a widespread phenomenon in the national government since the inauguration of John F. Kennedy.

The key zones of potential tension and conflict in agencies of this kind lie not between management and workers, though these are not absent; nor between management and professionals, because most of the management is professional; nor between professionals and workers as such, since many of the workers are professionals. Rather they are delineated by the lines (solid and dotted) running roughly vertical on Chart I. Specifically, they include tensions between:

(1) politically appointed officials and the elite profession (or its elite segment), especially if the political leaders are not members of the profession (or segment);

(2) different and competing segments of the elite profession;

(3) the elite profession (or elite segment thereof) and other professions in the agency, including especially those in line and administrative professions.

My unproven observation is that the most explosive situations in professionalized public agencies arise between those in different professions (or segments) and in different personnel systems who are approximately equal in level of responsibility and pay, but where one is "more elite" than the other. That is, the principal tensions are horizontal and diagonal rather than vertical. Personnel who are clearly subordinate are more likely to look upon their professional superiors as defenders and representatives than as opponents; and the professional superiors regard their own role in this somewhat paternalistic fashion. This is less true in programs staffed by unionized employees, and with the growing organization of public employees it may change substantially in the future. But unionization is only beginning to invade the professional agencies. A professional's status is not threatened by his secretary, his bookkeeper, or his janitor. He can, and often does, "go to bat" for them, and they may look upon him as their principal advocate. Not so other professionals in other segments and professions who are free to challenge his competence and his judgment.

Each profession brings to an organization its own particularized view of the world and of the agency's role and mission in it. The perspective and motivation of each professional are shaped at least to some extent by the lens provided him by his professional education, by his prior professional experience, and by his professional colleagues. These distinctive views are further molded and strengthened through internal training and experience in the agency itself; and where the professional corps within the agency is one of long standing, where it operates through a well-entrenched career system, and where there is a vigorously defended stratification between the professional elite and others in the organization, these post-entry forces can be very strong indeed.

The analysis of different public organizations in terms of their professional structure and intraprofessional and interprofessional systems of relationships is basic to the true understanding of their anatomy and physiology. Important decisions are likely to be the product of intraprofessional deliberation, representing the group views of the elite profession in the agency, compromised in some cases to satisfy the demands of other professions and non-professionals. Social relationships outside the office usually parallel professional relationships within. Members of the same profession in an agency are "colleagues," like professors in a university; and the flavor of their work is similarly collegial. Toward members of other professions, their behavior is likely to be more formal, sometimes suspicious and even hostile. Toward sub-professionals and other workers, the relationship may more frequently be paternalistic, patronizing, or dictatorial. Members of the elite profession identify their own work and that of the agency with their profession; the others are a little "outside," they are supplementary or supporting. The "climate" of an organization as well as its view of mission and its effectiveness in carrying it out are in considerable part a product of its professional structure.

THE PUBLIC EMPLOYMENT OF PROFESSIONALS

As the professional composition of public agencies has substantially revolutionized their internal anatomy, physiology, and nervous systems, so has the emergence of professions revolutionized the precepts and practices of public employment. Both revolutions continue with the development and solidification of new fields and new sub-specialties. Although there are large differences in precepts and practices among different jurisdictions of government, the basic directions in public service employment are clear. They also are probably inevitable. They apply to virtually all professional fields, whether or not under civil service laws. They are challenging, modifying, or overturning the most central—and most cherished—principles associated with civil service reform in this country: equal opportunity to apply and compete for jobs; competitive examinations for selection and (sometimes) promotion; "the job's the thing"; equal pay for equal work; neutral and objective direction and control of the personnel system.

These changes in practice, affecting a very substantial proportion of the public service and most of those groups which provide administrative leadership, have been going on largely unnoticed. Few have remarked about them—few even of the authors of books about public personnel administration. Yet the evidence is convincing.[15]

The most important of the changes is the last one, which involves the direction of personnel activities; it underlies the others. In general, what has happened (and is happening) is a *delegation* of real personnel authority, formal and/or informal, from a central personnel office or civil service commission to the professions and the professionals themselves.[16]

A basic drive of every profession, established or emergent, is *self-government* in deciding policies, criteria, and standards for employment and advancement, and in deciding individual personnel matters. The underlying argument for such professional hegemony is that no one outside—no amateur—is equipped to judge or even to understand the true content of the profession or the ingredients of merit in its practice. The argument is difficult to challenge, particularly in highly de-

15. My own evidence, some of which is summarized herein, derives principally from studies conducted during 1966 by my research assistant, Keith Axtell, of employment practices of federal, state, and local agencies in California. It is supplemented by studies in a few other places and by my own observations and interviews elsewhere.

16. The word "delegation" is not precisely accurate in a good many fields, since many developed pretty independently of any central personnel office, and there was no real *process* of delegation. But delegation is a reasonably accurate description of the product, whatever the nature of the evolution which preceded it.

veloped, specialized, and scientized fields with which an amateur—or a professional in personnel administration—can have only a passing acquaintance.

The means whereby the professionals assert their control over personnel policies and actions are many and diverse. Some are specified and required by law and/or regulation; others grow out of gentlemen's agreements within—or in spite of—general civil service laws; some reflect a silent abdication by the general civil service agencies or a failure to assume an effective role; and some are unintended (or mayhap intended) consequences of others. I shall discuss them under three headings: influence and control by the professional elites within governmental agencies; influence and control by "outside" professions and their organizations; and influence and control by institutions of professional education.

Professional Elites. The extreme examples of professional control within agencies are provided by the various commissioned corps in the federal government which have never been under a general civil service system. Here one finds the most consolidated mechanisms of internal control by the elite group and particularly by senior members—the *elite cadre*, as Janowitz termed it. They determine the standards and criteria for entrance; the policies and procedures of assignment; the appropriate work content of elite corps positions; the criteria for promotion. They also set up the machinery for personnel operations, usually including boards, all or a majority of whose members are drawn from the corps itself. They also superintend the policies and operations of personnel management for other employees, including other professionals, who are not in the elite, yielding as little as they must to civil service requirements, to the other employee groups, and to outside professional interests.

Much of this personnel control is sanctioned by law. It is significant that personnel matters in the various corps carry such preeminent weight and importance. Historically the handling of personnel was long entrusted in the Army to the staff division known as G-1 (A-1 in the Air force) ; today the first deputy chiefs of staff are responsible for personnel. In the State Department the Board of the Foreign Service has, since its founding, been essentially a personnel board, as the Director General of the Foreign Service has been primarily concerned with matters of personnel. It may be noted too that in these cases the professional elites have assumed control over the administration of personnel not in the corps: reserve officers, enlisted men (or Foreign Service staff), and civil servants.

Among the agencies not dominated by a commissioned corps, professional control over personnel matters has been less conspicuous but nonetheless effective. In many cases it is carried out under the canopy of civil service laws and regulations. The professional elites normally have the most influential voice in determining personnel policies, standards, and criteria within broad prescriptions of civil service law. The recent trend toward decentralization, both at the federal level and in other large jurisdictions, has of course facilitated this development. Personnel selection for professionals is in many places left to boards, which are usually dominated by agency professionals. As will be seen later, competitive written and performance examinations in most of the established professional fields have in many places been abandoned in favor of evidences of qualification determined outside the agency and indeed outside the civil service system. What is left—normally an "unassembled" examination of the candidates' records and/or an oral examination—is conducted by boards composed principally of members of the agency's elite profession. The same situation pertains to other personnel actions: assignments, promotions, disciplinary actions, etc. In most cases the central influence is that of the agency; and if it is controlled by a professional elite, the basic control lies with that elite. The civil service or personnel agency provides assistance in recruitment, a certain amount of professional personnel guidance, certain procedural requisites, and participation and perhaps inspection to ensure conformance with procedures. The substance of personnel policy and decision rests, however, in the professional elite.

Our studies (conducted in 1966) of employment practices of federal, state, and local jurisdictions in California in general confirmed the tendency toward professional elite control of policies, standards, and actions within the agencies in which the professionals were elite. There were, of course, variations in the degree of control and in the techniques whereby it was made effective. In general, these variations seemed responsive to two factors: first, the degree to which the professional group had established itself as truly elite within a given agency; and second, the degree to which demand exceeded supply for professionals in the field in question. The better established and recognized professions had greater control, and those in which supply was scarcest had greater control. We found this to be true at all levels of government in the employment of lawyers, natural scientists, engineers, doctors, social workers, and public health professionals. In the federal government, we found it true also for foresters, architects, and some others. In the state of California, it applied to psychiatrists in mental hygiene; among local governments, it applied in varying degrees to recreation, city planning, librarians, and some others.

The Professions and Their Organizations. Among the established general professions, the practice of registration or licensing of practitioners is an old one. Indeed, it is a common index of whether or not a profession is truly "established," and many of the aspiring newer fields are seeking registration to give them official and legal sanction. Registration of professions, like that of other occupations, is normally accomplished by the legal delegation of state powers to a board, itself normally composed exclusively or predominantly of members of the profession. Registration normally requires the passing of an examination, drafted and graded by the board or other professional group. In all of this, it should be noted, the civil service organization plays no part, and the examinations themselves are directed almost exclusively to the presumed knowledge and skills required for private practice, not to governmental policy and managerial problems nor, indeed, to those of large organizations of any kind. In well-established fields, such as law, medicine, dentistry, architecture, some kinds of engineering, and school teaching, licensing is normally requisite to practice at the journeyman level. In others, it is essential to advancement to higher levels of responsibility and supervision: accounting and nursing, for example.

Govermental agencies, other than the licensing boards themselves, play little part in the licensing process and have little influence upon or even interest in the content and standards of the examinations. Very probably the finding of James W. Fesler in his study, *The Independence of State Regulatory Agencies,* in 1942 is still accurate: "Professional licensing boards are virtually the creatures of the professional societies. . . ." [17] Yet it is clear that these examinations significantly affect the education and the qualifications which make for a professional man. The governments by and large accept those qualifications as gospel in their own employment. In some fields (e.g. law, medicine) registration is an absolute requisite to hiring at any level. In others, while not required, it may be sufficient evidence for hiring—without further evidence of qualification—and a basis for preferential treatment for advancement as well. Professionals who have gained their license credentials in most fields are likely to escape any further tests of competence and knowledge if they aspire to enter government employ. For them, the governments have abandoned to the professions themselves the testing of merit insofar as it can be determined by examinations of knowledge and skill. Further, it may be noted, the

17. Chicago, Public Administration Service, 1942, pp. 60–61.

licensing tests are non-competitive among the candidates. Qualifications are measured only in terms of passing a minimum standard—which may of course be a high one.

But perhaps most important is the effect of the licensing structure upon the content, the dimensions, and the boundaries of the individual professions. As Corinne Lathrop Gilb pointed out: "Public administrators generally fail to acknowledge *the extent to which the structure and composition of regulatory boards affect the division of labor and authority in the work world."* [18] And the "work world" of course includes the administration of government itself.

Professional Education.   Over the long pull the most profound impact upon the professional public services is that of the universities—their professional schools, their departments in the physical and social sciences which produce professionals, and their faculties in general. Higher education produces the bulk of future professionals. By their images, and by their impressions upon undergraduates, the schools have a great influence upon who opts for what fields and what kinds of young people—of what quality, what interests, what values—go where. It is clear too that they influence the choices of students among employers—whether government or other, and which jurisdictions and agencies of government. By their curricula, their faculties, their teaching, they define the content of each different specialism and the expectations and aspirations of the students in each. These students will of course include the principal operators in government tomorrow and the principal leaders the day after tomorrow.

In most professional fields governments have accepted, without much question or knowledge, the academic definition of content and the academic criteria of qualification and merit. Most governments, like other employers, rely upon

18. In her recent work, *Hidden Hierarchies: The Professions and Government* (New York and London; Harper & Row, 1966), p. 194.

accreditation; possession of the sheepskin from an accredited institution is enough. Accreditation itself is normally based upon a review and approval of a given school's program by a committee of a larger organization composed of, or dominated by, professional educators in the same field. It reflects a consensus among academics in a given field as to the minimal curricular and faculty requirements necessary for practice in that field. In most fields accreditation and high academic standing (grade point average) are more important to governmental employers than professional licenses. Where registration has been provided in only a few states (or in none) —as in social work, city planning, or librarianship —accreditation and grades become almost the sole criteria. Accreditation moreover is sometimes a requirement for licensing. Where government employers have any significant choice among candidates for jobs in the recognized professions, their reliance is placed upon (1) whether they come from accredited schools, (2) their grade point averages, and (3) the recommendations of professors. All three are of course academic determinants.

In the main, governments have yielded to the universities and professional educators the significant influences, the criteria, and the choices about public employment. Few of our larger governmental units give any competitive examinations on substance—that is, knowledge and skill—for candidates in professional fields. They leave it largely to the universities to determine what knowledges and skills are appropriate, and who among the graduating students are deserving of appointment. In a few fields, they also rely upon licensing examinations, themselves controlled by practitioners outside of government and/or professional educators. Among the agencies dominated by an elite professional corps, personnel decisions are largely dictated by the corps.

In this connection it is interesting to note that the Congress as recently as 1944 reaffirmed in the Veterans' Preference

Act its long-standing suspicion of formal academic qualifications for civil service jobs:

"No minimum educational requirement will be prescribed in any civil service examination except for such scientific, technical, or professional positions the duties of which the Civil Service Commission decides cannot be performed by a person who does not have such education."

The civil service has since excepted about ninety different occupations which comprehend virtually all the established professional fields, a great many emergent professions including some that are exclusive to government, and most of the natural, life, and social scientists. The omissions from the civil service exceptions are more conspicuous than the exceptions themselves. Lawyers are of course omitted since they are not under civil service anyway. Occupations in administrative fields, such as budgeteers, personnel specialists, purchasing officers, tax administrators, accountants, and administrative officers are not excepted. Urban planners, but no other planners, are excepted. None of the fields normally considered among the humanities at universities is excepted; among the social scientists, political scientists, public administrators, and historians are conspicuous in not being excepted from the Congressional fiat. (Anthropologists, economists, psychologists, and sociologists are all excepted.) The normal mode of entrance for those in non-excepted fields is the highly competitive Federal Service Entrance Examination. In the excepted fields, entrance is normally made without written examination. It hinges on a review of the college record, recommendations of professors, and, for higher level positions, experience.

The professional suspicion and opposition toward politics and government, suggested earlier, is probably even more vigorous among university professors. Here it is strengthened by the creeds of academic freedom and professorial autonomy. Apparently, the further one progresses through higher education the less he is enticed by governmental employment; [19] and this must reflect to some extent the influence of university faculties. Business administration was for a long time considered the principal competitor of the public service in the employment of the highest grade university graduates. Now both are suffering, not from each other, but from the universities themselves.

In this chapter we have come full circle. Near the beginning, we discussed the impact of the knowledge explosion upon our society; near the end, we discussed the impact of the universities upon public employment. The latter is a facet of the former. As knowledge has grown and as occupations have been increasingly professionalized, the public services have become more dependent upon the founts of knowledge, the universities. In their own organizations, governments have both reflected and influenced the occupational structure of the society. In so doing they have benefited tremendously through the advancement in the level of achievement in every field. They may also have suffered in the declining degree to which the central governments could control and direct operations in the general interest. For in the process, they have yielded a great deal of influence over *who* will conduct and direct individual programs, and how the content of programs will be defined as well.

For better or worse—or better *and* worse—much of our government is now in the hands of professionals (including scientists). The choice of these professionals, the determination of their skills, and the content of their work are now principally determined, not by general governmental agencies, but by their own professional elites, professional organizations, and the institutions and faculties of higher education. It is unlikely that the trend toward professional-

---

19. On this point, see especially Franklin P. Kilpatrick, Milton C. Cummings, Jr., and M. Kent Jennings, *The Image of the Federal Service* and the accompanying *Source Book* (Washington, D.C., The Brookings Institution, 1964).

ism in or outside of government will soon be reversed or even slowed. But the educational process through which the professionals are produced and later refreshed (in continuing educational programs) can be studied and conceivably changed. The needs for broadening, for humanizing, and in some fields for lengthening professional education programs may in the long run prove more crucial to governmental response to societal problems than any amount of civil service reform.

5

Three Systems of Merit

MUCH OF THE LITERATURE about public personnel lays such heavy emphasis upon the civil service and civil service reform that one may be misled to the impression that the public service consists of two elements: those employed under civil service laws and rules (the good guys) and the politicians (the bad guys). My own emphasis upon the evolution of a neutral civil service in Chapter 2 is similarly skewed, for it quite ignores the development of other parts of the public service which are neither political nor civil service in its traditional sense. These other parts comprise a majority of all public employment and include three of its biggest sectors: military personnel, school teachers, and skilled and unskilled labor.

In fact, it may be well at the outset to frame the entire topic in statistical terms. At the present time, more than one out of every six Americans works for a government—federal, state, or local. About one-quarter of these—4 per cent of the labor force—are officers or enlisted men in one of the military services. About three-quarters of all American civilian employees work at state and local levels of government, and half of these are in the field of education, mainly teachers. Neither the teachers nor the military are employed under civil service systems, nor are they typically "spoils" appointees; indeed, their personnel systems resemble each other more than they do the traditional civil service. There has of course been a recent and substantial increase in military personnel growing out of the Vietnam War. But the longer run trend of federal employment has been static or even slightly downward. State and local employment is rising rapidly and consistently and is expected to continue to grow for some time to come. Most of this increase is occurring in fields only partially covered under traditional civil service systems.

So it behooves us, if we are to gain a balanced picture of the whole public service, to look beyond the civil service type of system—as well as the patronage type of system—since both together comprehend only a minority of public personnel. The framing of a satisfactory typology of personnel systems, however, is a challenge. In the first place, American governments have displayed almost unlimited ingenuity in developing different kinds of arrangements for the employment of personal services, ranging from compulsion (selective service) to volunteers (Peace Corps, Vista, etc.) and Without Compensation (WOC), with a great variety of categories in between. Another difficulty arises from the distance one finds between the law and regulation on the one hand and attitude and practice on the other. There are substantial numbers of departments and agencies in state, county, district, and city governments which are under no legal civil service but still employ people in accordance with orthodox civil service practices. Conversely, there are departments and agencies at all levels of government which are legally under civil service whose employment practices bear little relationship to the traditional merit system.

For purposes of description, analysis, and comparison, it is useful to classify the public service into four main types of personnel systems:

1. *political appointees:* elected or appointed, below the level of chief executive, without tenure unless it be for an elective term of office;
2. *general civil service:* white-collar personnel, mostly non-pro-

fessional, who enjoy tenure, *de jure, de facto* or both, and whose employment is administered in accordance with traditional civil service practices with emphasis upon *the position;*

3. *career system:* white-collar personnel, mostly professional or para-professional, who enjoy tenure in agency and occupation though not in positions, and whose employment is administered as a progressive, preferably planned development with emphasis upon *the man* rather than the position;

4. *collective system:* blue-collar plus an increasing proportion of white-collar personnel (from categories 2 and 3 above), whose employment is governed primarily or in substantial part through bargaining between union or association and governmental jursidiction.

This grouping does not by any means comprehend all those people who make up the public service or all the methods whereby public servants are employed, but it does include most of those who have continuing impact upon public policy. The boundaries around each category are not clearcut, and they are moving. There are gray areas between one and another, particularly between the political on the one hand and both the general service and the career system on the other, and between the general service and the career system. There is unquestionably a tendency of movement from the general service toward the career service as high-level occupational specialisms develop standards, coalesce, and become recognized—that is, professionalize. There is also a growing movement from the general service and the career systems in the direction of the collective category as labor organization accelerates among white-collar workers.

In the descriptions and analyses that follow the four categories are treated, for purposes of clarity and emphasis, as extremes or, in Weberian terminology, as "ideal types." Yet none is "ideal," at least in terms of the author's system of values, and none, as presented, is "typical." The distinctions, if overemphasized, nevertheless are clear and important.

Each category has a different role, function, and influence in the larger governmental system; each operates under a different set of constraints and according to a different set of loyalties and identifications; and each is employed by governments according to its own set of proprieties and expectations. All are, or can be, "merit systems" if one accepts a liberal definition of the term. But the criteria of merit in the various categories differ widely in accordance with their role and mission in the polity. Each presents its own distinctive complex of problems for democracy.

It should be observed that the division of the public service into four categories does not by any means correspond with organizational differentiation. Most sizable public organizations include at least three categories (career service, general service, and blue-collar workers), and many include all four. This means, among other things, that for most public agencies there must be at least three different systems of personnel administration, even though all may be covered within the same set of laws and rules.

It should also be noted that the four categories do not represent vertical class distinctions, corresponding to and re-enforcing a four-class society, even though, by and large, the political officers probably enjoy the highest prestige and hierarchical power and the collective groups are probably the lowest in prestige though often well up the scale in terms of financial reward. Many in all the first three categories are educated at or beyond the college level, and all three participate in top level leadership. It is interesting to contrast this classification with that applicable to the public services in Europe which clearly derives from a social class division, operating through the intermediacy of the educational system (see Chapter 2 above).

The remainder of this chapter concerns the first three categories listed above. The general civil service and the career systems are juxtaposed for purposes of contrast, and a discussion of political appointments follows. The fourth category, the collective system, presents certain special problems for a democratic state and is considered separately in the following chapter.

CAREER SYSTEMS AND THE GENERAL SERVICE

Both the career systems and the general service system of public employment developed in this country, in part, in reaction *against* the political spoils system. Both are thought of as merit systems; indeed, members of career systems often view incursions of general civil service practices into their territory as violations of merit. On the other hand, the general civil service itself is often referred to as a career service, especially to contrast it with political appointments. Yet, historically and ideologically, the career system and the general service are a long distance apart. The two seem to be moving toward one another, as I shall develop later, although their differences in operations and in consequences remain significant and often vivid.

The origins and development of the general civil service system and the characteristics which derived from this history have been discussed in Chapters 3 and 4. Career systems have two types of origins, one ancient, the other relatively recent or parallel in time with the development of the general civil service system itself. The model of the old career system—the "ideal type"—is that of military officers of the Army, Navy, Air Force, and Marines. The most nearly "ideal" of the ideal type today is probably the personnel system of the officers of the line in the U.S. Navy. The military system has been copied in or adapted to a number of other federal activities—in fact, virtually all which employ commissioned officers: the Foreign Service, the Public Health Service, the Coast Guard. It has also been, in varying degree, a model for state and local police systems and for local fire departments, although in a good many of these it collided with the egalitarian philosophies of spoils and the civil service systems and was severely modified.

The underlying concepts of these older career systems, especially the military and the diplomatic, are rooted in distant history, long before the founding of the United States and at least as far back as European feudalism. Some sociologists have attributed the basic distinction between military officers and enlisted men to the feudal class distinctions between lords and vassals during the feudal era. As a matter of fact, it probably predates feudalism. Likewise the titles, prerogatives, and roles encompassed in the U.S. Foreign Service trace in some part to the formal relations between the heads of states of many centuries ago. Associated with such age is a rich body of tradition and a deep feeling of attachment on the part of members of the service toward the service itself, a feeling that approaches veneration. It is hardly necessary to observe that such a feeling is quite unlike that of the typical general service employee toward the civil service. In the one case the service is an *institution;* in the other it is merely a *system of employment.* Most of these older career services are identified with a single employing organization over which they have an historic monopoly of control. And in their self-image, they associate themselves with the service, not the organization, which they take for granted.

The difference in attitude is illustrated by one's response to a question as to what his occupation is. A non-professional civil servant working in the Department of the Navy is most likely to respond, "I work for the Navy Department"; an officer, "I am an officer (or an admiral or a captain) in the Navy." A recent questionnaire survey of Foreign Service officers asked exactly this question: how would you respond to a question asked by a stranger at a party as to what your occupation is? Half replied, "I'm a Foreign Service Officer." Another third responded either, "I'm in the Foreign Service," or "I'm in the diplomatic service." Only one in eight said, "I work for the State Department."

The more recent style of career system has attended the development of individual professions—new professions in response, primarily to new kinds of governmental programs, or specialized subdivisions of general professions, or members of general professions which have well developed professional career lines both in and out of government. The first of these types—new occupational fields which, at the time of their founding, were exclusively or predominantly employed by governmental agencies—are represented by various agricultural specialists, city managers, foresters, geologists, social workers, and city planners; the second—offshoots of established professions—by public health specialists in various fields, highway engineers, space scientists, etc. The third includes professionals performing their trade in governmental employ, but according to the career standards and processes of the profession itself—doctors, dentists, lawyers, architects, etc. Most of these, as they grow and develop their own self-identification within government, tend toward career systems of employment, distinct from the main body of unprofessionalized civil service and from the other career services.

In spite of substantial differences among the various professional fields, there are certain common denominators of concept and practice which are similar also to those of the older services, as exemplified by the various commissioned corps. These common denominators distinguish them from political appointees on the one hand and the general service on the other. In the paragraphs which follow are set forth the principal characteristics of career system ideology and practice which distinguish them from the traditional civil service under four headings: general attributes; operating characteristics in terms of personnel administration; consequences in terms of governmental decision-making, operations, and democratic control; and finally the challenges with which our evolving society is confronting them.

GENERAL ATTRIBUTES

The first attribute is really a definition. A career system is an employment system built upon a given specialization of preparation, knowledge, and skill for which one systematically prepares in his junior years, which provides his first major job, and which assures him a progressive employment in that line of work until his death or retirement. In government the assurance traditionally lies within a single agency or department; but as parallel opportunities are established in other jursidictions, careers may be pursued in comparable agencies in the same line of work. There is a stake on both sides—for the employee and for the employing agency—in the continuity of employment: the employer loses its investment of indoctrination, training, and experience if the employee leaves; the employee, to the extent that he has specialized his talents and experience in the agency, loses his marketability to other employers.

A second attribute of career systems is that there is a close identification between the system and the organization in which it operates. In fact, as suggested earlier, the personnel system supersedes the organization in the minds of the career servants. Elections and political leadership may come and go and organizational structures may be modified, but the career personnel system is likely to survive. It has been noted, for example, that it is easier to reorganize the Army than to bring about fundamental changes in the structure of the military personnel system. In general, the work of the career service in an organization is viewed as the work of the organization, especially by the accredited members of the system.

This view was colorfully illustrated in a (possibly apocryphal) story attributed to President Eisenhower when he presided over Columbia University. At a meeting with members of his faculty, Mr. Eisenhower alluded to professors as "employees of the University." A respected professor arose to correct him: "We are not employees of the University, Mr. President; we *are* the University." (In some ways academics are more nearly an "ideal type" of careerist than the line officers of the Navy.) Professors, like others in career systems, prefer to think of themselves as "members" of the system—

e.g. "faculty members"—rather than as "employees" of the organization.

There are two very significant corollaries to this identification of the career system with the organization *and* its objectives. One is the insistence on assignments of members of the system to the key line positions—that is, the positions with significant policy-making and decision-making authority. The members are pushed by this drive as high in the organization as is politically possible. This is of course precisely the same tendency we have already alluded to in connection with the professions. The second is the parallel drive to make the system self-governing as far as its personnel policies and decisions are concerned. Control of the criteria for entrance, for assignment, and for advancement and control of the application of those criteria is sought by accredited members of the system, quarantined as far as possible from outside (usually meaning political or amateur) interference. The same applies to other personnel activities; but in career systems especially, entrance, assignment, and advancement are the three key activities.

A third and related general attribute of career systems is the *interdependence of a system and its members.* Historically, the origin of most independent career systems may be traced to their monopoly character in the employment market. The Army was the only employer of Army officers, as were the Navy and the Foreign Service of their officers. This was largely true, in the beginning stages at least, of most of what are here called public service professions. Each required officers with particularized skills, abilities, and experience which could be gained only within the system itself. It may be noted that this is in direct contrast to the historic assumption of our civil service system that the schools and colleges and private employers could produce all the skills and knowledge required.

To a less pronounced extent, the same phenomenon has

occurred in agencies dominated by members of general (as distinguished from public service) professions. The qualifications for entry are the same as, and therefore are competitive with, those of other employers. But if it is true, or if it can be claimed, that advancement to upper level positions requires the kinds of experience that only *this* agency can provide, and if it can also be claimed that *this* kind of experience qualifies career system members for no other kinds of employment, the monopoly character of the employment relationship grows with the tenure of the members. This phenomenon contributes to a growing feeling of interdependence between agency and member which results in an actuality. The system will have invested a great deal of time, effort, and money in the recruitment of personnel and the new workers' development to journeymen and leadership status and cannot afford to let them go in their prime. On the other side, every journeyman member of the system will have dedicated a good share of his working life to the development of capacities not of particular value to other employers. Each—the system (or "organization") and its member—is dependent upon (or "stuck with") the other. This phenomenon has probably contributed to the relatively more *paternalistic* personnel practices of career systems: their greater concern about progressive assignments, about employee welfare (including the welfare of employee families), about employee development and training programs, and about fringe benefits, including generous retirement systems. Unlike most of the general service, a central problem of many of the career systems has been that turnover is *too low*, slowing advancement opportunities for the younger members. This has contributed to the lowering of retirement ages in these systems, and to the developing of devices whereby those failing of advancement may be *selected out* (retired prematurely) without prejudice and without great financial sacrifice.

The potential dividends deriving from the close relationship between a career system and its members are very substantial. They include a relatively high sense of *loyalty* and *devotion* of the members to the system; and insofar as the system is identified with the organization and its purposes, to the latter also. There is a greater sense of *discipline* to behave in approved ways; to work according to the professional standards of the career system; and to accept assignments and tasks which are difficult, disagreeable, and sometimes hazardous. Insofar as one is confident that those in decisive positions are associates with like orientations, experience, and ambitions, he is likely to feel confident that his own destinies will be directed knowledgeably and fairly. Finally, there is a basis in communication and language, in orientation and experience, in long-standing association, for mutual understanding and sympathy among members of the system—a basis for *team spirit*.

The sense of "oneness" between a career system and its members has probably been strongest in those agencies for which there is only a single employer in the nation; that is, in the monopoly employers such as the military services and the Foreign Service. But the same consequence occurs among many functional agencies in the states, cities, and counties where there is only one potential employer for a specialty at a given place and where most system members are unable or unwilling to move. In such situations there is a monopoly employment situation quite comparable to that of the military services.

Fourth, there is in a career system a heavier emphasis upon and recognition of *status* than in the general service, an emphasis reflected not only in the various activities of personnel management but also in the behavior, interpersonal relationships, and attitudes of those in the organization. Status in a modern career system is based more upon *ascription* than upon *performance;* but it is ascribed not in consequence of family or social status, as in medieval societies, but of *initial achievement* in education, specialization, and conquest of the obstacles at the gates of entry. Increasingly it depends upon superior (or at least successful completion of) specialized education at a university, sometimes evidenced by passage of an accrediting examination, appointment, and successful completion of a probationary period. But once the young candidate has "made it" he is "in the career." If he is employed in an agency in which his field of specialism is dominant, he has acquired *status* above others in that organization who lack these credentials; and, with respect to the work and problems of that organization, he has acquired status in the polity and the society in general. This is to say that in a career system ascribed status itself is achieved, not inherited, but once acquired depends rather little upon subsequent achievement beyond a basic and approved level of professional behavior and performance. Status gained in a given calling and organization is not automatically transferable to other kinds of activities and organizations and it is not equated with social status in society in general. A career system which is highly esteemed (including self-esteem) within an organization may indeed be little known or cared about in the outside world.

There is also heavier emphasis placed upon status *within* the career system itself to differentiate among its own members in a vertical pecking order. This is most pronounced and visible in the older career systems—the military where the symbols of rank are worn with the uniform, or the Foreign Service where rank determines seating arrangements at formal functions among many other things. But it is true too of the newer ones: of the various ranks of engineers in a state highway department, of foresters in the U.S. Forest Service, of faculty members at a university. Rank, once acquired, is a more important determinant of prestige and sometimes of influence than are position, current responsibilities, and performance.

Another kind of internal status differentiation is that which elevates certain sub-specializations within the system itself. This is very pronounced and pervasive in some systems:

officers with wings in the Air Force
line officers of the Navy
officers of the Corps of Engineers (In fact, there is a pretty well
     recognized pecking order among the various arms and
     services of the Army.)
political officers in the Foreign Service
civil engineers in a highway department
medical doctors in the U.S. Public Health Service

Such status valuations among specializations are best known to the members of the systems themselves, and they have many subtle—as well as some not so subtle—effects upon behavior, operations, and decision-making within organizations. Again, it may be observed that they may run directly counter to occupational prestige in the minds of the public. For example, lawyers in general have significantly higher public prestige than do engineers in general. But in the Army Corps of Engineers the engineers are not out-ranked by lawyers from the Office of the Judge Advocate General, nor are flying officers in the Air Force, nor line officers in the Navy.

PERSONNEL OPERATIONS

It is unnecessary here to specify in any detail the differences between the personnel practices of the general civil service and those of career systems: a broad-brush outline of the basic contrasts that characterize the approaches of the two types toward personnel decisions will suffice. Generalizing at this level is hazardous, for it invites a degree of exaggeration for purposes of emphasis; and the two kinds of systems are tending to become more alike, as will be demonstrated later. The differences between the non-existent "ideal types," however, are striking. Anyone who has observed two or more of them operating in the same organization—for example, civilian and officer personnel in any of the military services—will have recognized that a wide gulf separates them. This is the more surprising because personnel administration has to do in all public organizations with similar activities: recruiting and selecting and appointing new people, making assignments, developing skills, providing for promotions, handling separations, providing benefits, keeping records, etc. But the wide spread in the kinds of emphases put on these different activities, in the perspective from which they are approached, in the ways that they are done, make them almost unrecognizable as being essentially the same things from one service to another. The paragraphs which follow emphasize those features of career systems which contrast most vividly with those of the general service.

The central conceptual difference lies in the career system's thesis that *rank inheres in the man* and depends upon the level of his advancement through a systematic and competitive promotion system, as against the general service thesis of *rank in the job,* determined by its difficulty and responsibility. This is the underlying difference because, from an operational standpoint, almost everything else flows from it. Position classification became in the general civil service the pivot of virtually all personnel activities; in the older career systems, it was virtually unknown until World War II, and it still has rather little influence in some of them.

Recruitment by the career systems was initially from a rather select group of graduates from certain colleges (the Foreign Service) or nominees of Congressmen, usually from upper- and upper-middle-class families (as in the Army and Navy). More recent professionalized career systems have required degrees from appropriate professional schools and passage of professional examinations by licensing boards in the states. The expectation (and hope) of these systems has been that recruitment would be from young persons upon completion of their education to the bottom rung of the career ladder (which was still considerably above the bottom levels of the agency's employment) . Career systems have always resisted *lateral entry* to career status at intermediate and upper grades. The general service on the other hand deliberately avoided—and to a considerable extent still avoids —limitations upon applications due to age or formal education or level of job; it developed on an unspoken premise of an employer's market in which there would be qualified applicants for any type of vacancy.

The criterion of selection for career systems was (and remains) the potential of the candidate to develop in the system's line of work over his full career. In the general service, selection has been based on the candidates' promise to perform adequately in the job class which was immediately to be filled. It may be noted that both systems were and are competitive in fields in which there is an adequate supply of candidates, and both have departed from competitive methods where the supply is inadequate. But the underlying difference remains: one selects for a career, the other for a job. Further, career systems generally give more emphasis to, and are more rigorous about, probationary periods for new entrants to assure themselves that new appointees are properly oriented, adjusted, and qualified to develop through the full career.

Advancement in career systems from junior to full journeyman status is largely automatic, provided the employee has successfully completed his probationary period and commits no negative or disqualifying acts thereafter. But promotions above the basic journeyman level are based upon a scheduled, man-to-man review in which each member competes with all others at the same level, and without regard to specific job vacancies (though within general budgetary limits) . Candidates for promotion are (hopefully) protected from competition with outsiders. In the general service, advancements depend upon specific job vacancies at higher levels, are not restricted to one grade, may or may not be competitive, and are not protected against possible encroachments of outsiders. Career systems are much more careful and thorough in building systematic written records and evaluations of their members, primarily for decisions on promotions. Determinations about individual promotions are customarily made by boards consisting of other and superior (in rank) members of the system, sometimes supplemented by a minority of outside members and subject to a variety of reviews and appeals. Promotion is a very important matter in career systems, not one to be left to a personnel office, or a supervisor, or a competitive examination. Consequently the performance and the behavior of members of a career system are heavily conditioned by their expectations of the criteria the boards will apply in reviewing their candidacies.

Forward *personnel planning* has been more necessary and generally far more advanced in the career systems than in the general civil service, except in highly specialized areas where there was an obvious shortage of qualified personnel. This is true in two quite different dimensions: the *macro*-planning for the personnel of the system as a whole, and the *micro*-planning of the careers of individual members of the system. Systemwide planning for a good many years in the future is essential if the system restricts itself to entry at the bottom level. The nature and numbers of entries this year depend upon one's estimate of the needs of journeymen five to twenty-five years hence and of leadership personnel ten to forty years hence. Next year's budget and recruitment plan and assignment program depend less upon next year's prospective need than upon expected needs a long time in the future. Such a problem does not exist in the traditional general service, which is built on the assumption that one can fill his needs at any grade from the employment market with only slight delay.

There is an equal necessity in career systems to plan the careers of individuals in terms of both their assignments and their training, partly to satisfy the present and anticipated needs of the organization, partly to respond to the needs, interests, qualities, and desires of the individuals themselves. In well-developed career systems one finds—as he seldom finds in the general service—individual career plans, sometimes projected ten or more years in the future, comprehending nature and place of future assignments, periods off for training, systematic rotation and transfer programs, etc. And though none of the career planning and development programs has yet developed to the stage of rational perfection, most are well ahead of the customary general service practice of assigning a person to a job, where he sits until "something better comes along" or, if he is aggressive, finds and pushes himself into a better job. In career systems, assignments and movements from job to job are planned, scheduled, and progressive, whereas in the general service they are much more subject to chance and to the initiative and aggressiveness of the employee himself. Further, the career systems have in general been in the forefront of training and educational programs for their members, which are likewise planned, formalized, and frequent. Only in the last decade has the federal general service possessed even the legal possibility of systematic in-service training, and opportunities are even more limited in state and local jurisdictions.

SOME CONSEQUENCES OF CAREER SYSTEMS FOR GENERAL GOVERNMENT

Members of a career personnel system must always work with other personnel within the organization who lack comparable career status—be they clerical, manual, custodial, other professional, or political. To the extent that the system approaches the "ideal," to that extent is it exclusive and preferential vis-à-vis the other employees. When personnel are working together on the same things but under the operations of two distinct systems of employment, there is always the possibility—nay, the likelihood—of abrasion between them, especially if one claims a near-monopoly of the top jobs, dominating influence on agency policies, and preferential rewards. A price of the sense of unity, cohesiveness, and homogeneity within the career system itself is friction, difficulties of communication, and low morale with and among other personnel of the agency. In fact, this seems to be a nearly universal phenomenon within all organizations having clearly differentiated career systems. Compare, for example, the *standard* problems of relationships between:

career officers in military establishments, enlisted men, and civilians;

academic and non-academic personnel at universities;

career officers and non-career administrative personnel just about everywhere;

politically appointed officers and career leaders at the top.

It is more pronounced where the personnel under two different systems have comparable *levels* of education and experience but in different fields and bring to bear different orientations on the same problems and different views of organizational purpose.

A second consequence has to do with flexibility in the utilization of manpower to meet rapidly changing needs. Here the situation is paradoxical. A career system which contains a body of trained and experienced persons can readily adapt itself to certain kinds of changes *in the short run* through quick reassignments, transfers, even movements over thousands of miles. It is uninhibited by position classification and enjoys a degree of loyalty and discipline, sometimes legally enforceable, not common in the general service. But if it is called upon to meet sudden needs requiring different kinds of skills or to anticipate and prepare for basic changes in mission, rapid growth, or rapid re-education, it is very inflexible. Its supply of journeymen and leaders within the system at any given time is largely fixed because of its inhibition against lateral entry. Increases for the future must have entered the pipeline years before. The promises given to members of a progressive career through most of their working lives inhibit reductions-in-force.[1] Most of the agencies with career systems have therefore instituted devices for handling fluctuating needs with minimal disturbance to the central career—reserve officer systems, the general civil service, temporary employment, contract personnel, for example.

A third consequence is a relatively high premium on conformity of individual behavior with the norms and the mores of the system, and with the purposes of the organization as they are perceived and defined by the system. The forces pointing toward conformity begin well before appointment. The "image" of the service is framed in the home and in college, particularly in professional school. One's choice of a field of study is the beginning of self-recruitment. The actual selection process, conducted normally under the direction of experienced career system members, should weed out those who are unlikely to conform; indeed, in some fields that is its primary purpose, for knowledge and ability are taken for granted on the basis of college degree and passage of professional examinations. Following appointment, most new members undergo a systematic training and orientation (indoctrination) course, followed by a more or less extended intern and apprentice program. Again, the nonconformists can be weeded out before their probation ends, while those who remain have better learned the norms and expectations which will frame their living and working style in the future. Thereafter there is the continuing pressure of supervision by older men in the service and association with colleagues, reenforced if necessary by the risks and rewards of efficiency ratings and the promotion system, all controlled by senior colleagues in the system.[2]

1. Many of the career services do not even have policies and procedures to govern staff reductions. But the selecting-out procedures of some of them are used for the purpose.
2. For a particularly perceptive analysis of how these processes operate in one career system, see Herbert S. Kaufman, *The Forest Ranger: A Study in Administrative Behavior* (Baltimore, The Johns Hopkins Press, 1960).

The "perfect" career man in the "ideal" career system, then, thinks, acts, and decides like his fellows; he is a "type" and is often so described. His responses are expectable. He is technically efficient in the field of activity of his career and according to criteria set by the system. He is a supporter and if necessary a defender of the system as the system is his supporter. He is likely to seek and to find technically correct solutions to problems, even though the problems may themselves involve elements not contemplated in the technique —that is, political or social or interpersonal. Where the problem is patently non-technical, his instinct is to withdraw and avoid "sticking his neck out." He is also prone to avoid or withdraw from open disagreements, hostility, and aggressiveness in his associations with his colleagues; internal confrontations threaten both the system and its individual members.[3]

A final consequence of career systems is *conservatism* in the sense of resistance to change that might weaken the system. I hasten to add that the conservatism of which I speak applies principally to threats of change to the system itself, to its status in the governmental world, and to the destinies of its members. Some career systems, like some professions, may be politically liberal and amenable to change.[4] Some indeed are in the business of inventing and bringing about change— as, for example, those in research and development laboratories or college faculties. Yet with regard to the *institution* of their employment relationship, even these are conservative

3. In an interesting recent report by Chris Argyris on Foreign Service officers and other officers in the State Department, the contrasts between the career and the non-career officers are described in very comparable terms—and are almost as overdrawn as this paragraph about the "ideal type." Argyris finds the "living system" of the Foreign Service officers, "dominated by a low interpersonal openness, levelling, trust, confrontation; a high withdrawal, mistrust of aggressive, fighting behavior; and a blindness to the superior's negative impact on his subordinates." *Some Causes of Organizational Ineffectiveness Within The Department of State* (Washington, D.C., Department of State, Center for International Systems Research, 1966), p. 25.

4. For example, compare the *political* stance of public health officers with doctors generally, or of public foresters with those in private employ.

if they have stabilized and established themselves as career systems. Among the older career systems, there is a generally conservative bias toward the subject-matter with which the members of the system deal. This is a product of the constraints against nonconformism and initiative that might be threatening to the system. It is a product also of the way the system operates to produce its leaders. The average age of the top career leaders in most public agencies today is around fifty years. Most of those in career systems will have spent most of their working lives in a single occupational field, many in the same agency. The holding of such a single perspective for so long a time—up to forty years—is almost inevitably a sculptor of viewpoints, values, and methods. Insofar as the leaders can impress upon subordinate system members their own views of the world—and as we have seen, the system itself provides effective tools for this—the older perspectives will dominate.

My treatment of the "ideal type" of career service above is admittedly extreme and overdrawn. There are probably no systems for which it would be accurately descriptive. One reason for this lies outside the personnel systems themselves: forces in society have prevented career systems from reaching their idealized image. They are not "closed" systems. Moreover, contrary forces have compelled the general civil service to move in the direction of career systems. There is thus a tendency for the two to draw closer together, so that neither clearly fits its classical description.

The General Service. We have already observed (in Chapter 4) the tendency of sectors of the general civil service, as they become self-consciously specialized and scientized, to frame themselves more and more as separate, self-contained, professional services. In addition, the general service outside the specialized careers has displayed a tendency to take on some of the accoutrements of careerism and to relax the rigorous application of "rank-in-the-job" and position classification. This tendency has been most marked at the bottom and entry rungs of the public service ladder. Thus the various general entrance examinations for young college graduates which have developed over the last three decades are designed to attract and select on the basis of career promise, not of specific qualifications for the first job. New recruits normally go through a training and/or intern program and are also advanced rapidly on a scheduled basis to the journeyman level (usually GS 11 or GS 12 in the federal government). To that point there is little significant difference between the general service and the career systems. Position classification, even beyond these early stages, has been considerably relaxed in various ways: greater recognition of the incumbent's influence on the job; employment of the two-track system of classification and promotion to make possible advancement of scientists in technical, nonadministrative work; broadening and generalizing of classes; etc. The concepts of career planning, progressive assignments, in-service training and development programs are finding their ways into general service systems; and the idea of the Senior Civil Service, which would itself have been a career system at the top level, has generated a good many modifications in the federal government and some of the states in the treatment of those in executive levels. It may be noted that most of these changes, actual and proposed, have been in the direction of recognizing rank in the man rather than rank in the job.

CHALLENGES TO CAREER SYSTEMS

All the older career systems—and particularly the commissioned corps—have been under considerable strain for many years, more especially since World War II. All have changed in response to pressures from outside and within, though sometimes reluctantly and bitterly; and all are in difficulties today. The major challenges fall into four main classes: egalitarianism, the knowledge explosion, management, and politics.

In their basic structures the commissioned services, particularly the military and foreign services, survived the drive toward *egalitarianism* which characterized much of the nineteenth century and had such impact upon the general civil service. Their staying power may have reflected in part the strength of example and precedent from other nations, partly the fact that their principal bases of operations were separate from the rest of American society. The relative exclusivity of the corps was supported by geographic separation. Through the nineteenth century and until World War II, the Army and Navy officer groups were dominantly of upper class or aristocratic origins. The great majority were, surprisingly, drawn from rural and small town settings. The South was heavily overrepresented. The division between officers and enlisted men and the importance of rank in both categories were visible, sharp, and distinct.[5] In the Foreign Service the great majority—both before and after the Rogers Act of 1924—were drawn from upper- and upper-middle-class families, mostly residents of the East Coast, and most were alumni of a handful of Ivy League colleges.[6]

In all the commissioned services the structure of the status system remains, but all have had to yield in a great many ways to the demands for *equal opportunity* and *equal treatment*. During and following World War II, as college level education became more and more available to middle- and lower-middle-class citizens, the recruitment base broadened; opportunities for moving from one (lower status) category to another were opened up and lateral entry was occasionally permitted—or even mandated under pressure from outside the system. Further, extreme differences in the conditions and privileges of the different personnel categories were attacked and considerably reduced. One common device was the setting up of new career systems, more or less modeled on

5. On these points, see particularly Morris Janowitz, *The Professional Soldier,* op. cit. Chapter 5.

6. See for example Warren Ilchman, *Professional Diplomacy in the United States, 1779–1939* (Chicago, University of Chicago Press, 1961).

the elite system and with comparable benefits and promises for advancement. Thus non-commissioned officers became a career in the military services; the Foreign Service Staff became a career in the State Department; nurses and social workers acquired their own career statuses in hospitals; and the non-academic personnel of universities were encompassed in something like career systems. (It is interesting and suggestive that no one has been able to invent a more adequate designation for "non-academic" personnel; almost their only common attribute is negative: they are *not* in the academic career system. Of course the same is true of "non-commissioned officers" in the military services.) A consequence of these developments has been the establishment within organizations of whole series of career systems, in many respects comparable with each other but distinct and in some degree separate. And in all, the central, original system remains—and struggles to remain—*elite,* the first among (not quite) equals. It retains, as far as possible, the key jobs with regard to organization policy; it controls, as far as possible, the operating personnel policies of the other career systems; and it monopolizes, as far as possible, the incumbency of the top positions.

In short, egalitarianism reached our older career services about a century later than it did the general civil service. It still has a long distance to travel, but the issue has been joined and there have been a good many changes.[7] What seems most surprising is the resiliency of the ancient feudal stratification in our career services; no rational observer from Mars could understand, or find any reason in, the trifurcated personnel structure of the Defense Department (officers, enlisted men, civilians). Neither could he understand how the trifurcated organization of Army, Navy, Air Force, each with

7. There are surprising likenesses between the recent and current efforts to reform (or "democratize") our military and foreign services and contemporary reforms of the civil services in some European countries, such as France.

its own ground troops, air forces, ships, missiles, and research and development programs, could exist in an era of missiles and guerilla warfare.

A second major challenge to the career systems, new and old, has arisen from the *explosion of knowledge,* both technological and social, since World War II. They have confronted essentially the same problem in this regard as have the professions in general (Chapter 4). No system built on the premise of bottom-level entry can equip itself internally with the vast array of knowledge and technique to handle, in an effective and up-to-date manner, the problems in its established arena of activities. Further, the growth of knowledge forces fundamental changes in the concept of what that arena actually is and what the system's public mission is. Problems which point up emerging dilemmas abound in almost every area of public activity: police confronted with racial turmoil; school teachers with their classes filled with underprivileged, future delinquents; diplomats involved in the development of new and only partially civilized countries; Army officers fighting a war they are not allowed to win; Air Force pilots working on projects which will make their wings meaningless; highway engineers seeing their products result in greater congestion. The growth of knowledge has made it apparent that the objectives and the subject-matter of most of the career systems relate to the underlying problems as effects and symptoms, not as core issues. Careerists must work with others in other systems of employment; they must accommodate their own patterns of thought and their own self-definitions to the requirements of collateral systems; and they must equip themselves with knowledge, skills, and points of view which are not provided through the older and traditional training, recruitment, and experience.

The responses of career systems to these kinds of challenge have varied widely. In general they have been conservative and defensive, giving an inch at a time; and by and large they have been less successful here than in their accommodations to the drive for egalitarianism. The strategies of accommodation include:

1. *redefinition of mission,* but this is effective only when accompanied by revisions in content of training and experience for newcomers and new types of training for those already on the job (illustrated by the Public Health Service, some branches of the military, some mental hospitals).
2. *providing for employment of needed specialists not provided by the career system itself in other categories of employment*—if need be in parallel career systems. (This has probably been the most common device. It maintains the "integrity" of the system and, hopefully, the system's dominance of the organization. It is illustrated in the hiring of civil service scientists in the National Institutes of Health, the reserves in the military departments, the Foreign Service Reserve, lecturers and research scientists at universities, and more or less permanent consultants.)
3. *subdividing themselves into specialized sub-career systems while retaining a common cement of doctrine and focus*—such as "leadership" among military officers or "diplomacy" in the Foreign Service.
4. *contracting out to other organizations, private and public, projects and tasks which the personnel of the service is not equipped to perform.* (This is of course best illustrated in research and development, but applies in varying degree to a wide variety of other activities.)
5. *absorbing into the "career" different types of specialization and experience by lateral entry.* (In the stronger systems this is a last resort which often must be forced from the outside. Lateral entry is of course a threat to the essence of the system itself. The Foreign Service is a most striking example. Its Wriston program of the mid-fifties was forced upon it, and both before and since, it has successfully resisted integration with foreign assistance and development personnel, with overseas information personnel, and with others.)

The failure of a career system to accommodate to growing knowledge and changing requirements—to redefine its self-image and take steps to give reality to a new one—may lead to a slow and agonizing decline in its control over and its influence upon the arena in which it operates. This has happened to some degree in a good many of the diplomatic services of the world, not excluding our own (though here the Wriston program halted the decline, at least temporarily). It is very probable that it is occurring now in a good many public welfare departments across the country in the face of the changed view of welfare and of the poverty program. The challenges to career systems deriving from the knowledge explosion and the accompanying changes in conception of problems, technological and social, are a specially intensified case of the broader challenge of modifying institutions to keep up with the accelerating dynamics of our culture.

The third kind of challenge to career systems is implicit in the emergence of *management* in public organizations. This is partly a product simply of growth in size of a great many public agencies. More important, it results from a growing realization of the complexities and the ramifications of consequences of public policies and decisions. Few of the career systems and of the professions, established or emergent, which comprise them, gave much if any attention to management (or administration) either in their preparatory education or in their in-service career and training programs. Yet students of administration have known ever since Henri Fayol that the bulk of activity at the upper levels of any given organization is managerial, not technical or professional. At and near the very top, technical knowledge and understanding are perhaps an essential instrument, but the basic content of the job is managerial in its broadest sense. Recent studies of public executives have re-enforced Fayol's argument; and they have shown that management is today much broader, more difficult, than the POSDCORB of the thirties. Our public executives today are dealing with problems which go far beyond either supervisory leadership or technical proficiency; they concern the social, economic, and political—as well as technical—consequences of governmental activity. *Management is also policy.*

It is not coincidental that career systems customarily derogate the word and the practice of administration. In the military, it is equated with the filling out of morning reports; in the Foreign Service, with the hiring of local personnel; in a university, with the treatment of stenographers. I recently heard a president of a great university say, "I like to think of myself first of all as a professor." I have heard comparable self-evaluations by military officers, public health officers, Foreign Service officers, and others—all at the top managerial levels in their jurisdictions. The "substantive" content of the career system is the valued element; management (or administration) is regarded as a routine, non-discretionary instrument. At the University of California, Mario Savio did not arouse much argument from the professors when he asserted that the job of the administration was to keep the sidewalks clean.

But the career systems are increasingly challenged—and increasingly vulnerable—in this position. A public health officer can hardly defend his position and status by citing his reputation as an M.D. or by noting that as an intern he delivered a dozen babies when his problems concern the pollution of the air, the remedies for atomic exposure, the problems of the underprivileged in the kindergarten, and most particularly the mobilization of a variety of resources, public and private, to meet these problems. Except for their widely different subject-matter content, there is little to distinguish the essential problems of the top-level public health officer from those of the welfare director, the military commander, the career ambassador, the highway commissioner, or the dean or president of a university. All are professionally oriented, all are concerned in problems which go far beyond their subject-matter training, experience, and interest. In the future fewer will be able to respond to public and political demands with the argument that they are *only* doctors, *only* welfare workers, *only* highway engineers, *only* military officers, *only* diplomats, *only* professors, *only* school superintendents and principals. They will be expected to be something more, and the more successful among them will be those who respond positively to that expectation.

The responses of the career systems to the growing importance and widening dimensions of management have, by and large, been grudging and slow. They have included:

1. separation, specialization, and demeaning of "administration," distinct from "substance";
2. establishing what amounts to a "two-track" channel within the career system, one occupying executive and managerial posts, the other engaged with substantive work of the system (e.g. Janowitz's distinction between "heroic leaders" and "military managers," [8] or the increasingly recognized distinction between "scientist administrators" and practicing scientists);
3. bringing in "experts" in managerial fields but in sub-career systems or in the general service, while maintaining direction and control by system members over their activities;
4. introducing general social and managerial considerations and criteria into the system itself—in education, selection, training, assignments, promotions, etc. (This seems usually to be a last resort.)

The fourth challenge to the career systems, which is here labeled the *political challenge,* is in a sense a summation of the others (egalitarianism, the knowledge explosion, and management). For politics has provided one of the principal vehicles—sometimes the final and decisive one—whereby the others are articulated and effectuated within career systems.

In its narrow sense, politics is and always has been the natural enemy of career systems. Most of these grew up in op-

8. Op. cit. especially Chapter 2.

position to and defense against political intrusion. Politics constitutes a standing threat, even if usually quiescent, against the very elements which are most central to a system's values: security of members' status and tenure; self-government; standards of entry as well as the policy against lateral entry; standards for advancement; and so on. One might hypothesize that those career systems which are best established, most widely recognized, and grounded in the most esoteric fields of knowledge are least endangered by politics. But none is completely protected all the time and under all circumstances.

If we define politics broadly to include those processes whereby interests and influences are mobilized and articulated to change or defend public policies and programs, its importance for career systems in relation to democracy is great. Large and important areas of policy are of course within the purview of individual agencies that are largely dominated by members of career systems. The development and effectuation of changes in policy thus inevitably depend upon the abilities, perspectives, values, and strategies of political leaders who are not themselves "of the career." There is a wide variety of channels through which advocates of change can operate: legislative investigations and consequent publicity; legislative committees and their staffs; executive task forces and other study groups, usually composed largely or entirely of members, public and private, who are not in the career system directly affected; legislation; executive directives; appropriations; and appointments not alone of political overseers of the career system but also of career members themselves to leadership positions.

Yet major changes in direction may often be successfully resisted and frustrated by a strongly entrenched career system which opposes them, even if in opposing it leaps the hurdles of laws and budgets and executive orders. The naming of a policy or a program does not make it live. Indeed, new policies depend heavily, in both development and effec-

tuation, upon the co-operation and support of the career
system and particularly of its leaders. Frustrated advocates of
change are likely to turn their attention—after a few failures
—to an attack upon the recalcitrant career system itself, its
leadership and its established modes of operating. It seems
likely that most significant changes in career systems have
originated outside the systems themselves or from threats
and fears of outside action. They include the broadening of
the recruitment base; the insistence upon admitting to membership in the "club" persons with different types of background and orientation; the revision of promotion systems;
and the reduction in distinctions and privileges between the
elite members and other employees within the same agency.
They include also the practice of dipping down into the system by political officers to select for leadership posts career
officers who are sympathetic to the aims of the political
leadership and who may also be "unorthodox" system members. Examples are found in President Roosevelt's selection
of General Marshall, and later in the selection by both of
them of such men as Eisenhower and Bradley; and further
in the choice by virtually every President of many Foreign
Service officers of less than top rank for ambassadorships and
for high posts in the State Department. The refusal of the
Senate to act on the Navy's promotion list until the name of
Admiral Rickover was added is an excellent example of the
use of a secondary political power to attack the fabric of a
career system's promotion policy.

Career systems, of course, are not exactly powerless against
this kind of attack. Many of them carry a great deal of prestige in the eyes of the public and in political circles. Most
have strong friends in both executive and legislative
branches, and a few command the support of enormously
powerful interest groups.

Most of the time, too, they have running for them the negative force of inertia. It is much easier not to change than to
change, and only occasionally can a head of political steam be

built up for "reform" of a system. They are most vulnerable in times of emergency for their agency, sometimes following a dramatic failure, and during a period of political transition following a change of party control through election. The first is illustrated by the military systems preceding and during a war; the Foreign Service during diplomatic crisis; welfare, police, and schools after a Watts catastrophe. The second has been abundantly illustrated following the election of an Eisenhower or a Kennedy, a Reagan, or a Lindsay. These turnabouts were times of trouble for many career systems.

The Political Appointment System

A principal potential instrument of change for career systems and for the general civil service is through appointment of outsiders presumed to be responsive to the wishes of the elected executives and legislators in power. I refer here to those whom the literature now describes as *political executives,* who may be simply defined as any appointee outside a protected civil service or career system who has policy-making duties.[9] They comprise in the national government the secretaries, undersecretaries, and assistant secretaries of departments; the administrators and their assistants in most of the non-Cabinet agencies; the members of boards and commissions; the chiefs of a significant number of the major bureaus and services; and a considerable number of subordinate officers presiding over divisions and other offices. The estimated numbers vary, depending upon one's liberality in defining "executive"; but it probably approximates 1200, of whom nearly half are appointed by the President and half by his appointees. Civil service law and practice vary so widely among state and local jurisdictions that it is hazardous to generalize there, but it is safe to assume that most of the larger governments in industrialized areas have political executives

9. The definition is adapted from that of Marver H. Bernstein in *The Job of the Federal Executive* (Washington, D.C., The Brookings Institution, 1958), p. 10.

in approximately parallel capacities and with comparable roles. Some have a great many more proportionately than the national government; some have many fewer.

It may well be that the political executives are *the* crucial element in the maintenance of democratic control over a public service which is increasingly professional and "careerized." They are, or can be, the true nexus between politics and administration.

There is so much variety among political executives and among the processes whereby they are employed that it may be stretching a point to refer to political appointments as a system. Basically the appointees have in common only that they have no insurance in their jobs and that a good many of them, particularly those at higher levels, are unlikely to survive an election which overturns the party in power. Many do not want or expect to stay in their positions, and this expectation of temporariness is shared by others in the agencies. Yet in the total governmental picture they do constitute a kind of system. Recruitment and selection are becoming increasingly regularized; there are discernible trends in the nature of the men and women chosen for these positions; and the summation of the widely varying roles of political executives is that of an imperfect but indispensable connecting link in the processes of public decision and operations.

There are of course wide differences in the types of people tapped for political appointments in different jurisdictions; yet one can identify certain broad patterns and directions which are common among the larger and more progressive ones—the national government, the industrial states, and the big cities. Most of what follows is based upon the national experience, which is the best documented, but it probably applies with only slight modifications to jurisdictions such as the states of New York, Michigan, and California, and the cities of New York, Chicago, and Philadelphia.

In the first place, there is growing emphasis upon brain power, declining emphasis upon purely political experience and reward. The Johnson administration is an extreme case, but only two of his Cabinet members in 1966 had had active political experience whereas six of them had been college professors at some time. This contrasts with the mid-nineteenth century when nine of every ten Cabinet appointments were lawyers—then nearly synonymous with politicians. At the second level—the assistant secretaries and deputy agency administrators—the recent study by Mann and Doig [10] revealed that during the Kennedy administration nine-tenths were college graduates, and this proportion had risen with every administration since Roosevelt. More than half had graduate degrees. The Warner study of federal executives indicated that the political appointees, who included many at the third level—below the assistant secretaries—were on the average better educated than civil service, military, and Foreign Service executives, and of course all of these groups ran far ahead of the general public in this respect.[11]

Second, in terms both of education and prior experience, there is more emphasis upon generalized backgrounds at the upper levels—Cabinet members and undersecretaries and assistant secretaries—than among political appointees below them. The latter are likely to be eminent leaders in specialized fields associated with the service or bureau to which they have been appointed. The former are more often educated in social sciences or "social" professions such as law and business administration, and many have had widely varying experience. Of 108 assistant secretaries intensively studied by Mann and Doig, only 30 per cent were appointed on the basis of "expertise," while nearly 70 per cent were appointed for their "general experience." Although political considerations entered into some of the appointments, less than 10 per

10. Dean E. Mann with Jameson W. Doig, *The Assistant Secretaries: Problems and Processes of Appointment* (Washington, D.C., The Brookings Institution, 1965).

11. W. Lloyd Warner, Paul P. Van Riper, Norman H. Martin, Orvis F. Collins, *The American Federal Executive* (New Haven, Yale University Press, 1963).

cent were chosen because of "service to the party." In other words, the appointment system at the Cabinet and the sub-Cabinet levels aims primarily to provide generalists rather than either experts or professional politicians.

This is partly a consequence of the organization of the national administration. Most departments and agencies are not structured along vocational lines. We have no Cabinet departments of education for educators; public works for engineers; welfare for social workers; health for doctors; mental hygiene for psychiatrists; science for scientists; police for policemen. The only exceptions are the Department of Justice, clearly for lawyers, the Department of State for diplomats, and the Department of Defense for the military. There are a few non-Cabinet agencies which parallel occupational specialisms—the National Science Foundation and the Council of Economic Advisers, for example. Most professional identification occurs at subordinate levels of service, in the bureau and division. It may be noted that the organizations of most state and local administrations are much more closely related to professional and occupational specialisms; and this may explain, at least in part, why in civil service states the politically appointed *generalists* are relatively fewer in number and smaller in influence than in Washington. It may also explain why their governors and mayors are relatively weaker, in relation to their administrations, than the President, and why their administrations often behave less responsively to general political forces.

A consequence is that, whereas at lower federal echelons political appointees include substantial numbers of professionals in both public service and general professions, the Cabinet and sub-Cabinet include relatively few except in law. It is highly significant that the proportion of lawyers (about one-quarter) is slowly declining. Of the other professions, only college educators have any significant representation; indeed, the virtual absence of some of the largest fields —notably engineering, science, and medicine—is striking.

Yet there is some evidence—perhaps I should say danger —that Cabinet and sub-Cabinet political appointees are becoming increasingly professional in their backgrounds and orientations. Mann and Doig emphasize the unusual degree of mobility reflected in the prior careers of these appointees and the emphasis upon presumed versatility in their selection. On the other hand there is heavy and apparently increasing reliance upon prior governmental service in the appointments; between 1933 and 1961, four-fifths had had some experience at the national level, and one-third had devoted the major part of their careers to the federal service. Though practices varied widely among different agencies, recruiters for political appointments clearly sought persons with experience considered relevant to the agency—either professionals promoted from the civil service or career system, or "professional-amateurs" with prior experience in the appropriate service or with outside experience considered relevant. Thus

the *State Department* depended heavily upon Foreign Service officers and officials with prior experience in political or career jobs in State or Defense;

the *Defense Department* relied heavily upon prior military experience and work as executives in large business establishments;

the *Treasury Department* emphasized banking and legal experience;

the *Justice Department* leaned of course on lawyers, with a genuflection to political considerations.

Practice in the other departments, which administer most of the nation's domestic programs, has varied widely, but one's general impression is that of a sporadically growing reliance upon relevant prior experience including particularly work in related sectors of the public service.

Unless—or until—political appointees at these upper levels are a good deal more professionally identified with the career elites of their agencies, they will provide substantial protection against narrow professional and career domination of governmental programs. Their education, their background, and their orientation and values are significantly different from those of the career personnel, whether civil service or career system. Their education is more general with stronger liberal arts flavor; their experience is more varied as to employer and field of work; their orientation is more likely to be toward that of their political superiors than of their career subordinates. They offer some assurance that considerations other than those of career professionals will condition administrative decisions and they thus contribute to a more effective and active representation of the interests of the whole people than would a service totally dominated by specialists.

In the passive sense, however, the upper-level political executives are not very representative. They are distinctly an upper-crust group. Their parents are in the higher income brackets; their education, as already noted, is very advanced compared with the rest of the population, and a high proportion were educated in the Ivy League institutions; a relatively high proportion hail from metropolitan areas. (This contrasts strikingly with the rural and southern backgrounds of many in the elite of the military services.) Clearly many of the upper level political positions in the national government have regained—or in some cases retained [12]—the aristocratic flavor of the early decades of the Republic. Of course the nature and the membership of the aristocracy have changed (if indeed the word is any longer meaningful), and the social distance between it and the middle classes has diminished. But that Cabinet, sub-Cabinet, and comparable posts still command high prestige in the society is evidenced by the kinds of persons who have accepted such appointments, often

12. For example, most of the Cabinet and a few of the ambassadorial posts overseas seem to have commanded high prestige and desirability for the well-to-do throughout most of our history.

in the face of considerable financial sacrifice, family inconvenience, and the expectation of hard and sometimes unpleasant work.

In respect to democratic responsibility, political executives at the upper echelons offer a balance to the career public servants, though in widely varying degree. In the controversial domestic areas particularly, most political appointees may be expected to reflect the general views of the chief executive or department head who appointed them.[13] Once appointed, the possibility of removal or transfer offers some assurance of loyalty toward the objectives of the executive and often to him personally. The appointments of a newly elected chief executive of a different party have a high symbolic importance as representing in deed what has previously been expressed in words. "By his appointments shall ye know him." They also have considerable operative significance. An Eisenhower or a Reagan will almost certainly turn to individuals with a relatively more sympathetic attitude toward private enterprise (whether or not businessmen themselves) than will a Kennedy or other liberal Democrat. In the Department of Agriculture, both parties draw heavily from the farm organizations and the food processing industries. But the Republicans give greatest weight to the conservative Farm Bureau Federation and conservative business leaders; for the Democrats, it is otherwise. The same applies to most of the domestic departments and agencies. Curiously, there is far less partisan difference in the appointments to the Defense and foreign affairs agencies, even to the top secretarial level. This is probably because since World War II there has been rather little fundamental difference with respect to these areas in the policy views of the dominant wings of the two parties. Both parties have drawn heavily

13. Principal exceptions are those in effect nominated for political reasons by legislators through senatorial courtesy, whose allegiance may be more to the legislator who engineered the appointment than to the executive branch.

upon the same recruitment sources and to a surprising extent
upon the same men. In these areas there have also been more
bipartisan appointments than in any other.

A much stronger orientation to professional and career
values is found in the political appointments to the third
echelon in the federal government—the bureau chiefs, the
heads of specialized offices, the Schedule C appointees. In
progressive state and local governments too, the professional
cast is usually among the upper echelon appointments. Here
the appointing authorities are less likely to respond to demands for either practicing politicians or generalists. Rather
they seek recognized and preferably eminent leaders of the
professions and sciences which are elite in the different agencies, whether they be public health doctors, psychiatrists, me-
teorologists, penologists, physicists, agronomists, economists,
civil engineers, educators, or librarians. The principal qualification is established reputation in the appropriate occupational field.

A second qualification—which may be primary in politically volatile fields—is basic sympathy and compatibility with
the policy objectives of the administration in power. In controversial fields, the incumbent political appointee may appro-
priately consider his tenure as temporary, unlikely to survive
a party transition. But most political appointees to superin-
tendence of professionally oriented agencies come from long
and successful experience in the profession; for a good many,
all of that experience has been gained in career service in the
agencies they are called upon to govern. And not a few of
these, once they have attained the preeminent position in
their agency, retain it until retirement, regardless of the
political vicissitudes during their unprotected terms. The
strength of professional support renders it dangerous for a
political executive to remove from office a respected professional leader—as President Eisenhower learned in connection
with A. V. Astin of the Bureau of Standards and as Governor
Reagan learned in connection with President Clark Kerr of

the University of California. In neither case was the incumbent protected by civil service or other guarantee of tenure; both removals were entirely legitimate. Yet both were attacked on the grounds that they constituted political interference with scientific or professional integrity. In contrast, one may observe how seldom a president or governor or mayor is criticized for replacing the top political executives who are not identified with a respected specialism. This we expect.

The third echelon political executives thus occupy a middle ground between the first and second echelons and the careerized agencies. In comparison with the former they

are more apt to be drawn from the career or civil service of their agencies,

are, in the great majority of cases, respected professional leaders in the specialism appropriate to the agency,

have a longer tenure expectancy in their job and almost complete confidence of continuing work in their field of specialization,

are more likely to view their role as one of representing the views and interests of their agency and its objectives and specialism,

are less likely to respond to change initiatives from political leaders, above and outside,

have an intimate acquaintance with their agency, its leaders and workways, and, on the other hand, view politics and political leadership with reserve and suspicion.

Many of these non-career executives at the third echelon epitomize their careerized agencies and personnel; they are eminent figures in their fields, principal representatives and defenders of and spokesmen for the services which they superintend.

Yet their stance differs from that of the permanent services below them. They *can* be replaced, or their situations can be made so uncomfortable as to induce them to resign or at least to alter their behavior. As noted earlier, political appointing officers, even when constrained to select bureau chiefs from within the agencies, can usually find individuals sympathetic with their general political views. It may be supposed that every career system and every agency harbors some dissidents and some non-conformists.

* * *

This chapter has analysed and contrasted three systems of employment: the career system, the civil service system, and the political system. Most of the larger public agencies contain at least two of them, and the majority contain all three. Each provides somewhat different types of persons, orientations, perspectives, skills, and knowledge. Each has its own distinctive view of responsibility, of representativeness, and of what constitutes the public interest.[14] The interplay among them may be the most interesting and crucial element in America's political democracy—especially near the top where decisive issues are negotiated, debated and resolved or tabled.

There is little agreement as to what kinds of positions should be covered within which system and what roles and powers their incumbents should exercise. Most of them have developed without a discernible rationale, and there is wide variation in personnel systems among different jurisdictions of government and among different agencies within each. The dangers of any system passing outer limits are clear. Where political appointments invade too far the provinces of the careerized services, there is a threat to substantive effectiveness, an invitation to inefficiency and even scandal. Where the political appointees are driven out, there is a threat to the general interest in favor of special interests, to "the public" in favor of a self-directed or entrenched bureaucracy. American history provides abundant examples of both types of dangers.

All the systems bring a certain kind of yeast to the dough of public management. The permanent services provide the advancing knowledge and technology, the responses to clients,

14. Though, as indicated above, in these respects the third echelon political appointees probably resemble the careerists more than they do the first and second echelons.

the more intimate acquaintance with program needs and operations. The first- and second-echelon political appointees bring fresh views on social needs, responsiveness to political and party leadership, and, in varying degree, a restless desire to question, to change, and to improve. If a working combination of the two is difficult to achieve, it is nevertheless fundamental to the forging of an effective public service under democratic direction and control.

6

The Collective Services

THE FOUNDERS of civil service did not bargain on collective bargaining. The polemics about civil service reform included no reference to employee organization; they were in fact antithetical to the idea of collective relationships among employees. There was, and there remains, an intense individualism in the civil service ideology. Each competitor should be measured against others by the yardstick of merit. In consequence, our governments operate today with little experience, little understanding, and little legal basis for dealing with employees collectively through organizations.

At the time of the Pendleton Act and of many of the state civil service laws which followed it, labor organization had little viability and enjoyed generally low repute; it was not a significant element in public personnel management. To be sure there had been unions in some of the military establishments half a century earlier, but these were minor and were not recognized in the civil service laws. In subsequent years labor organizations blossomed and flourished, particularly in the Post Office. But public management—and the ethos of civil service reform—by and large opposed them. Appointment and advancement in the civil service were to be based upon individual merit, and the criteria were not to be adulterated by pressures from associations of employees.

Until quite recently the prevailing posture of the administrative side of most American governments has been indifferent or hostile to labor organizations, and indifference toward organizations seeking to exercise influence may be just as damaging as hostility. Few private employers have so successfully and so long resisted effective collective bargaining as have most governments. Until the 1960's, almost every national administration opposed effective labor organization within government, even while some of them deemed it desirable, even mandatory, in the private sector. Indeed, the Janus-like perspectives of a good many of the liberal political leaders on the labor issue during the first six decades of this century were remarkable. At the same time that they were championing the rights of organized labor in industry and commerce, they were ignoring or denying them in government. Thus could the earlier Roosevelt issue his notorious "gag" rules in 1902 and 1906 forbidding employees or employee associations to "attempt to influence in their own interest any [pay or] other legislation whatever, either before Congress or its committees. . . ." The later Roosevelt, sponsor and signer of the "Magna Carta of American Labor," the Wagner Act of 1935, two years later wrote that collective bargaining "has its distinct and insurmountable limitations when applied to public personnel management. The very nature and purposes of government make it impossible for administrative officials to represent fully or to bind the employer in mutual discussions with government employee organizations." [1] No president since the thirties could publicly espouse a repeal of the rights of labor in the private sector to organize and bargain. Until John F. Kennedy, however, none had taken any serious steps toward comparable assurances for public employees; and, as will be noted later, Kennedy's action in 1962 fell a good deal short of labor's guarantees in industry.

This contradictory stance is paralleled by another curious paradox. The cause of organized labor in government is both defended and attacked on the grounds of democratic princi-

1. In a letter of August 16, 1937 to Luther C. Steward, President of the National Federation of Federal Employees.

ples. On the one hand the rights to associate, to organize, to exercise such power (subject to certain ground rules) as can be commanded to improve the workers' lot—these rights are held to be inalienable in a democratic polity. On the other hand public employee organizations, it is alleged, pose a threat to democratic rule; to the extent that they can advance the interests of their members they deprive political representatives, who are responsible to the whole people, of power over public policy. Further, an effective government union or employee association can hardly be neutral on some public issues, nor can its members. Finally, and in most extreme form, a state representing a sovereign people cannot bargain away that sovereignty to single groups of its citizens in their own interest. In a democratic polity, policy and administration must ultimately be unilateral from the top down—or bilateral, if one realistically considers the executive and legislature as separate powers. At any rate, it is not trilateral. So the argument runs.

The rationale seems to be currently losing its relevance. The pragmatics of American history have a habit of brushing aside legal niceties in the rush of events; they have proven again and again the plasticity of constitutions and laws. We are today in a tornado of governmental labor activity, comparable to the storm that swept the private sphere in the thirties. In some ways, the most intriguing question is: Why has it come so late? What has held it up? Government—more especially the federal government—has often aspired to be a "model employer," in the vanguard of fair practices in the employment field. And not without effect. It led most employers in the competitive principle, "equal pay for equal work," a retirement system, a decent minimum wage, and more recently non-discrimination, employment of the physically handicapped, and equal employment opportunities for women. But with respect to the recognition of labor organizations and truly effective bargaining, the federal as well as most other American governments are about a generation late. They have some catching up to do.

The Heritage to 1962

In the state and local governments, unionization and collective bargaining were little developed until quite recently. In some, the employees never won the battle for security in tenure against political spoils. In others, civil service became so strongly entrenched as to inhibit the development of powerful employee unions. In most, unions were discouraged by the essentially conservative cast of state legislatures, city councils, county boards, and boards of education. Unions did, however, develop in certain parts of the federal establishment, and until about 1923 they had a growing influence on federal employment policies. Starting in the Post Office soon after passage of the Pendleton Act,[2] the postal unions played an important part in the passage of the eight-hour-work-day law for federal employees in 1888 and later, of the Lloyd-LaFollette Act of 1912, which remains the most important—indeed almost the only—law asserting and protecting rights of federal unions. Later joined by a service-wide union—the National Federation of Federal Employees (NFFE)—the unions were influential in the passage of the Retirement Act of 1920 and the Classification Act of 1923.

Subsequently union influence seems not to have grown except in certain pockets of the federal service. Federal unions have contributed support to a number of measures designed to strengthen the merit system and benefit civil servants (such as the Welch Act of 1928, the Postmaster Act of 1938, the revisions of the Retirement Act, and a variety of fringe benefits and pay acts). They have also dampened a number of efforts to damage the civil service. Their aims were fundamentally *simpatico* with civil service; like the career systems, they

2. The first permanent union in the Post Office, the National Association of Letter Carriers, was formed in 1888.

shared with civil service the common enemy of patronage. Civil service provided a guarantee of tenure and security and an orderly, predictable system for personnel decisions. Government unions therefore worked within the civil service system, contributed their support to its extension, and sought to maximize their influence in the civil service organizations. Few of them were in any sense radical.

In some organizations the unions came to exercise great influence on employment practices. Largest among these (and probably still the most important) was the Post Office with its tremendous, widely scattered, and politically influential labor force, the great majority of whom have long been unionized. Second were the industrial establishments of military and a few other agencies where the craft unions of the private sector have long been active. Third were a few federal agencies in which management deliberately encouraged unionization and collective bargaining. Notable among these is the Tennessee Valley Authority.

Yet for the bulk of federal employees outside the Post Office Department, employee organization was weak if not totally unknown. There was no positive sanction for collective bargaining, and management was more often negative about it than encouraging. President Kennedy's Task Force in 1962 reported that one-third of all federal employees belonged to labor organizations—a proportion almost exactly equal to that of non-agricultural employees in the private sector. About three-fifths of the federal union members were in the postal service, and more than half of the others were blue-collar workers. Obviously the unions had made only minor inroads among the main body of white-collar federal employees outside the Post Office—something in the order of 15 per cent.

This apparently low level of unionization in the federal government is illusory. White-collar employees are not widely unionized in the private sector either. Employee organizations have not thrived in the service industries, and much of government is service. On balance, one would guess that among comparable groups of employees (blue collar, clerical, professional, and administrative), unionization of federal employees is no less the general rule than it is in private organizations.

In fact, the extent of unionization at the federal level was surprisingly high, all things considered. Government unions lacked the collective bargaining guarantees of a Wagner Act; most of them disavowed the use of the ultimate weapon—the strike; few could assure prospective members of effective influence upon the central issues of labor relations: wages and hours. Despite these handicaps, unionization of federal employees was equal, in proportion, to that of private employees in comparable categories.

If union membership in federal employment was equivalent to that in the private sector, the acceptance of collective bargaining was not. Mrs. B. V. H. Schneider attributes this not to any theory of sovereignty or other peculiarity of public employment, but to a simple behavioral fact: "At no time have a sufficient number of federal civil servants believed that bargaining rights were desirable or necessary and been prepared to press for such rights." [3] The statement is no doubt true, but it does not explain *why*. I would hazard as one reason that the bulk of federal employees are professional or clerical, and these categories have nowhere been aggressive in collective bargaining until very recently. A second reason is that the middle and lower grades of the federal service have, on the whole, done pretty well with their wages, hours, and fringe benefits without the necessity of labor organization. For political reasons, and perhaps partly as a spin-off from the aggressiveness of the postal unions, personnel in the lower levels of the federal service have for many years been in a favorable position relative to other employees. Their pay has been relatively high, their hours reasonably low, their vacations relatively generous, their positions secure. The incentives for

3. "Collective Bargaining and the Federal Civil Service," *Industrial Relations*, V. 3, 3 (May 1964), p. 98.

unionization and collective bargaining in such circumstances would almost certainly be minimal. The personnel who are relatively disadvantaged in federal (and much state and local) employment are those in upper level professional, scientific, and administrative positions, mainly because of the well-known compression of salary rates. They have not been disposed to organize (until quite recently) in either public or private employ.

A third reason is found in the linkage of labor organization in the public mind and among prospective union members with its more extreme weapons, particularly the strike, coupled with the general fear and disapproval of their use against "vital" public activities.[4]

In any case in 1962 there was a relatively quiescent public labor movement in most of government, one which—with sporadic exceptions—made modest demands and little public noise. Effective systems of collective bargaining, systems in which both parties had sufficient power to influence settlements, were few and far between.

THE CURRENT LABOR EXPLOSION

Against so sleepy a backdrop, the accelerating development of labor organization and collective bargaining in government in recent years has been both sudden and unexpected. It has probably been fed in part by the rapid growth of state and local employment, in part by the increasing disposition of sub-professional and professional personnel to organize and endeavor to improve their lot. But behind it also has been the fundamental anomaly of governments' supporting and requiring practices in the private sector which they discouraged or denied for their own employees. In the words of the American Bar Association in 1955:

"A government which imposes upon private employers certain obligations in dealing with their employees may not in good faith

---

4. Though Leonard White showed long ago that many services in the private sector were as vital as some in the public—or more so. (See his "Strikes in the Public Service," *Public Personnel Review*, January 1949.)

refuse to deal with its own public servants on a reasonably similar basis, modified of course to meet the exigencies of public service." [5]

Changes began, as has so often been true of public reform movements in the past, at the municipal level. Several of the larger cities piece by piece negotiated agreements with unions of various kinds and coverage during the fifties and early sixties: Philadelphia, Cincinnati, Hartford, Detroit, New York, and many others. In 1959, Wisconsin by state law launched its now-famous program authorizing and prescribing methods for collective bargaining in cities (though not in the state itself) and providing that a state agency, the Wisconsin Employment Relations Board, supervise its operations. The Wisconsin system is probably the nearest approach in the nation to that provided by the National Labor Relations Act for private employees.

The federal government came along a little later. In fact, Congress had under consideration, in every session from 1948 on, one or more bills which would have recognized federal employee organizations. Most of them, including those introduced in the 1950's by Congressman Rhodes, would have guaranteed collective bargaining with relatively severe penalties to administrative officers who infringed on such rights. Lacking administration support, the bills made no headway. One of President Kennedy's early actions was to establish a task force to study and make recommendations on labor-management relations in the federal service. In his memorandum setting up the task force, the President made it very clear that in his view federal employees had a *right* to organize and to bargain; and by his appointments to the task force, including particularly then Labor Secretary Goldberg—long counsel to the CIO and the Steelworkers Union—as its chairman, he made it clear that he expected an approach fundamentally similar to that in private industry.

5. *Second Report of the Committee on Labor Relations of Governmental Employees,* 1955, p. 125.

The basic thrust of the task force report and of the Executive Orders [6] which in January 1962 gave it effect was hardly unexpected. Though bills have since been introduced in Congress to give legislative sanction to the system and to strengthen it, the Executive Orders remain the principal government-wide statement of policy and charter of operations for employee organizations. They provide a decentralized system of bargaining in the departments and other agencies under general guidance of the Civil Service Commission and accord exclusive recognition to all unions chosen by a majority of employees to represent them. As will be seen later, the orders fell several laps short of the rights and procedures long standard in private industry; in particular they provided no supervisory and appellate agency in any sense comparable to the NLRB.[7]

Nevertheless, the Kennedy orders were a significant shot-in-the-arm for labor unions in the federal government. The number of employees represented by exclusive unions has grown steadily to over a million in mid-1966. This was nearly a 50 per cent increase over 1964, and constituted almost 40 per cent of the federal civilian work force. More than 90 per cent of these employees were covered under negotiated agreements. It should be noted, however, that the great majority were concentrated in a relatively small number of agencies: 60 per cent in the Post Office Department, more than 25 per cent in the military departments, principally the Navy. Outside of the heavily unionized Post Office, about 33 per cent of the blue-collar workers in the executive branch and 14 per cent of the white-collar workers had exclusive representation.

Perhaps the more striking effect of the federal action of 1962 was the impetus it gave to unions and bargaining in state

6. Executive Orders 10987 and (principally) 10988, January 17, 1962.

7. A board is provided. It includes the Secretary of Labor, the Chairman of the Civil Service Commission, the Secretary of Defense, and the Postmaster General. This would compare with an NLRB constituted of the chairmen of the boards of General Motors, U.S. Steel, AT&T, and Standard Oil of New Jersey.

and local governments, particularly local. In numbers of employees, these are the fastest growing sector of the entire American economy, expanding at about twice the rate of the rest. They are also now the fastest growing in the rate of unionization. The American Federation of State, County, and Municipal Employees multiplied its membership between 1956 and 1966 by three and a half, and in another decade could become one of the largest unions in the nation with more than a million members. Increasingly professional employees, who traditionally abhorred labor organization, have formed and joined unions—teachers, nurses, social workers, engineers. And increasingly have public employees in local governments gone on strike, often in defiance of clear statutes banning strikes against government and court injunctions against them.

The growing size of public employee unionism is matched by a growing militancy. Legislators have haltingly, often reluctantly, yielded to union demands by adopting bills accommodating to them and providing experimental systems of labor relations. By 1967 sixteen states had passed laws authorizing or requiring collective bargaining procedures in their local governments, and these included many of the larger industrial states—Wisconsin, Connecticut, Minnesota, Michigan, Massachusetts, and New York. Some of these go far beyond the existing federal procedures in labor relations.

The current explosion of labor relations in government comes at a time when the proportions of craft and blue-collar workers are declining and professional and sub-professional employees are rapidly rising. Its most significant elements may in fact be among the professions. It comes at a time too when the labor movement in the private sector is in doldrums, barely holding its own and, as Walter Reuther has suggested, in serious need of new and more ambitious aims. As one scholar in labor relations has written: "The 1960's have already earned the right to go down in labor relations history as the decade of the public employee . . . the rise of these unions is the most significant development in the industrial relations field in the last thirty years." [8]

Is Public Service Different?

In the social sphere it often takes theory and principle a long time to catch up with practice and "common sense." Scholars and most of the rest of us have long accepted the proposition that public employment is different from private, that the approved norms of the industrial sphere cannot apply to civil servants. The argument was usually buttressed by a number of reasons, among which sovereignty was central. The growing public-private mix of social enterprise through a vast array of mechanisms makes it difficult to draw lines, as the rising aspirations of workers make it difficult to differentiate rights and expectations of workers in public or private employ. The current rapidity of change makes observation unreliable, prediction very risky. The paragraphs that follow undertake no theoretic analysis of sovereignty and the rights of labor. Rather, they are meant to elucidate the practical problems in the governmental realm of labor organization and collective bargaining that are visible today and that demand resolution in the future. One thing is clear: civil service and collective bargaining are different. They arise from different ideologies, espouse different aims and values, pursue different procedures. But how are they to be reconciled?

A first category of problems centers on the question: *What is negotiable?* The National Labor Relations Act prescribes for the private sector bargaining in good faith over "wages, hours, and other terms and conditions of employment . . ." —a blanket stipulation which has been interpreted to cover a very large portion of the labor front. In most American governments at every level, hours, most wages, and some other conditions are determined by a legislative body, not by man-

---

8. Jack Steiber, Director of the Michigan State University's School of Labor and Industrial Relations, as quoted by David R. Jones in *The New York Times,* April 2, 1967.

agement. There is legal doubt as to which and what part of these prerogatives a legislature *can* delegate away (though practice differs among different jurisdictions and among different kinds of employees in the same jurisdiction). In the national government, salary scales for the bulk of employees [9] are established by law and can be changed only by law. The same is true of most large jurisdictions. This means that unless the employee organizations bargain directly with the legislatures, their negotiations with management on salary levels can be advisory at the most, for the power to make decisions lies elsewhere. Management cannot make commitments in this field, which constitutes the central issue of most labor activity. Unions could, theoretically and indirectly, affect salaries on a selective basis through negotiations on position classification. But if there is any sacrosanct element in public personnel administration, it is the integrity of the classification plan, objective and free from pressure. Can classification be made negotiable without shaking the roots of civil service itself?

As a matter of fact, other conditions of employment are often legislated, sometimes in such precise detail as to leave little or no discretion to administrators: criteria for appointments and promotions, hours of work, vacations and other leave, retirement, reductions in force, fringe benefits. It is significant too that most of the causes that employees pursue cost money. Almost everywhere in American governmental life the appropriating power resides in legislative bodies— city councils, school boards, county boards of supervisors, state legislatures, Congress.[10]

It is of course possible for legislatures to delegate powers to

9. Exceptions are the blue-collar workers known as wage-board employees, whose wages can be, and in fact are, negotiated in a limited sense; i.e. against the criterion of the prevailing rate.

10. There are exceptions, especially in the semi-autonomous, self-supporting enterprises such as the Port of New York Authority. The Tennessee Valley Authority is very nearly in this category, and this may have been a necessary condition for the success of its collective bargaining system.

administrative officials to negotiate some matters, subject usually to later ratification and financing, although the constitutionality of such measures might be doubtful. Otherwise it would appear that comprehensive bargaining would require direct participation by the legislatures themselves. This appears to be feasible in some, perhaps most, local jurisdictions, and is now standard practice in Wisconsin cities. But "bargaining" in the state legislatures and in Congress is surely dissimilar to NLRB-type negotiation; it more nearly resembles standard interest-group tactics.

In addition to this legislative problem, there are constraints on the administrative side which limit the area of employee negotiation. Some of these, not unlike those that weighed on the rugged individualists in the private sector three decades ago, relate to the powers and responsibilities of public management, its accountability to the people, its exercise of sovereignty. Others stem from the ideology and procedures of civil service. To the extent these are detailed in law, there is not much labor can do beyond accepting them or going to the legislature to seek changes in the law. As one city manager put it: "Perhaps most important [of the differences between public and private employment] is that public administrators do not have the same freedom of action which their counterparts in the private sector enjoy. Their authority is conferred on them by public law and by the definition of that law is limited and cannot be delegated or contracted away." [11]

In retrospect, the Kennedy orders of 1962 now seem a mild step toward collective bargaining because of their concern for the rights of management. They decreed that federal agencies have no duty to bargain over areas of policy such as "the mission of an agency, its budget, its organization, and the assignment of personnel or the technology of performing its work." And they preserved to management the rights:

"(a) to direct the employees of the agency, (b) to hire, promote,

11. Elder Gunter, City Manager of Pasadena, California, in a letter in *Public Personnel Review,* January 1966, p. 57.

transfer, assign and retain employees in positions within the agency, and to suspend, demote, discharge or to take other disciplinary action against employees, (c) to relieve employees from duties because of the lack of work, or for other legitimate reasons, (d) to maintain the efficiency of the government operations entrusted to them, (e) to determine the methods, means and personnel by which such operations are to be conducted, and (f) to take whatever actions may be necessary to carry out the mission of the agency in situations of emergency."

It should be observed, however, that substantial rights are reserved to management in private industry, and that individual federal agencies can permit, and have permitted, some or many of these subjects to be covered under collective bargaining agreements. Experience has shown that, even within these limitations, there is an impressive array of subjects that are negotiable.

Clearly, the push of public employee organizations as they grow stronger will be toward exercising greater influence on personnel activities heretofore considered non-negotiable and retained within the unilateral prerogatives of civil service commissions and other public personnel agencies. Indeed, this movement is already well under way in some places. The City Personnel Director of Milwaukee, a city with a well-established labor relations policy, probably spoke for most of his colleagues in the public personnel field when he wrote: "Personnel people should be prepared to resist pressures by employee organizations to encroach upon these areas of traditional but proper merit system concern." [12] "These areas" included appointments, position classification, establishment of minimum examination requirements and class specifications, and promotions. But if these issues, together with others in the legislative domain, remain "off limits" to labor representatives, what is in their domain will not likely satisfy them and their union members much longer. Grievance procedures and working conditions, not covered by law and the tradi-

12. Robert C. Garnier in a letter to *Public Personnel Review*, ibid. p. 53.

tional merit system, constitute a foot in the door; but the door to effective collective bargaining in most public agencies is a long way from being open.

In comparing labor activity in the public service with that in private, a second category of problems concerns the *tools or weapons* which employee organizations may use. Here, too, there are vital historic and ideological differences, but many of these are now under union attack. Labor organization and collective bargaining were themselves frowned upon in government for most of our history, and they are still forbidden in some jurisdictions. The strike, the anchor power of most unions outside of government, is still forbidden in the national government and a large number of states. Compulsory arbitration of unresolved disputes is now possible in a very few places, but it was conspicuously omitted from the Kennedy orders. The closed or union shop was likewise denied; it is probably one of the most difficult of labor's potential tools to square with the principle of equal treatment, long the central tenet of America's merit systems.

In the federal government, employee organizations have recently won the right to negotiate, to reach written agreements with management, to represent employees in grievance cases, and to have union dues checked off from payrolls. But they lack most of the kinds of weapons to back up their demands that are available to kindred organizations in private employ. In some local jurisdictions and among some kinds of employees the ultimate weapon, the strike, has been utilized, whether or not legally, without severe penalty. In fact, strikes among local employees are sharply increasing. There were 38 in 1962, 42 in 1965, and more than 150 in 1966. Some of them —of transit workers, school teachers, social workers, nurses— have been large and dramatic. It appears likely that local bans against strikes in the public service will gradually erode, at least among many of the largest categories of government employees. But such a development at the federal and state levels will surely come much later, if at all. The federal ban on strikes—it makes them a criminal offense—has very seldom been defied; but on the whole it does not appear to be under serious challenge, even by the more aggressive labor leaders. In fact, many seem to regard it as a necessary safety valve in the event of particularly damaging strikes in the private sector, which the national government can terminate through the process of nationalizing a whole industry.

But labor in the public sphere has political weapons not generally available in the private sector. It can and does carry its problems to legislatures and legislative committees. In the federal government and in the large industrial states it can usually expect sympathetic consideration of its views, and through affiliation with larger sectors of the labor movement it can pack a considerable political punch. Reapportionment of state legislatures may enhance this influence. A major reason that strikes on the local scene have increased so sharply is that local legislative bodies in most jurisdictions have been predominantly conservative. At the national level and in the industrialized states, legislatures are at least as amenable to labor organizations as are the executive branches.

In short, the powers and weapons of labor unions in the public sector are different from those in the private. They are primarily political rather than economic. At the local level the absence of legislative responsiveness has in many places forced employee organizations to utilize the weapons of unions in the private sector. But even there, the major weapon, the strike, is essentially a political one. One need not judge whether labor organizations have been more or less effective in the public service than elsewhere, or whether employees have been better treated in government than outside. But clearly their instruments for betterment are different, and it seems reasonable to expect that they will continue to be different.

In comparing collective bargaining in the public and private sectors, the third question is, *who negotiates for whom?* On the employee side, the situation in government is not unlike that in the private sector thirty years ago. There are many different types of organizations operating from different principles with different aspirations, and often they are at war among themselves. They include unions affiliated with the labor movement; unaffiliated unions; craft unions, usually comparable to and affiliated with the same crafts in the private sector; industrial-type unions (like the American Federation of Government Employees and the American Federation of State, County, and Municipal Employees); general employee associations (which are commonly likened by unionists to company unions in the private sector); and professional associations. In general, governments seem to be moving uncertainly and sporadically toward the principle of exclusive recognition, long established in the private sector. But uncertainties remain about the definition of the bargaining unit, the handling of situations in which no organization commands a majority, the inclusion of supervisory officials within bargaining organizations, and other issues. With a few exceptions the employee associations—strongest in some of the states—have supported and worked through normal civil service machinery. The industrial-type affiliated unions have been most aggressive and have posed the gravest threat to accustomed public employment practices. Recently, professional associations and unions of professionals in a number of fields have bitterly contested their powers to represent the interests of their professional groups. The unionization of professionals is a relatively recent phenomenon in both the public and the private sectors, and the problems seem to be roughly similar in both.

The question of who will represent labor thus seems not greatly different in the public and the private sectors, except that the former is running several decades behind the latter in crystallizing the issues. One would guess that, in most fields below the professional and supervisory level, affiliated unions will gradually assume primacy as they have for the most part in private industry. Among the professional and sub-professional employees, whatever the outcome of the current struggles between unions and associations, clearly the former are driving the latter toward more aggressive demands and tactics, including strikes.

A difference even more difficult and crucial concerns the question of who will represent the employer—i.e. the government—in employee negotiations. As we have seen above, the problem here arises first from the separation of powers between executive and legislature. It is complicated, secondly, by the varying degrees of identity and autonomy of individual public agencies, with respect to both the executive and the legislature. Thirdly, the role, power, and degree of autonomy of the civil service organization are a source of ambiguity. Our experience to date at all levels suggests that labor organizations, as they acquire self-identity and recognition, are not greatly influenced by the niceties of political and constitutional theory. They approach the sources of real authority through whatever devices are most promising of results. If present trends toward larger and more influential unions continue, particularly at lower levels of government, we may expect increasing—and increasingly direct—demands upon local legislative bodies. Insofar as these demands are frustrated, the unions will turn to state legislatures to provide guarantees of negotiating rights, minimum standards, and mediating and appellate machinery. Within limits, legislative bodies may delegate, and in many cases have delegated, negotiating powers to administrative officers and special agencies. But the possibilities of appeal back to the legislature can hardly be foreclosed for any organization with potential political power.

It seems entirely possible that one effect of growing unionization of local employees will be increasing centralization of control over local government labor relations by state legislatures. Such a result is particularly likely where the one-man, one-vote reapportionment results in a liberalization in legislative membership.

The Dilemma of Civil Service

The rapid growth of labor organizations, like that of the professions, is clouding the already hazy role of civil service agencies. Historically the agencies were the protectors of the public service against the machinations of politics; later, the defenders of efficiency as well as security in the management of public personnel. Public employees turned to them in both roles as their principal spokesmen and as proponents of employee interests. The more recent position of some civil service agencies as a service arm and an instrument of management has caused employees and their growing organizations to re-examine their relationship with the agencies. The trend toward legal recognition of employee organization and of rights to collective bargaining confronts them with grave and as yet unresolved problems. Are they properly instruments of management with whom labor organizations should negotiate (short of legislative appeal)? Or are they properly representatives of employees in seeking benefits, participation, and adjustment of grievances? Or are they properly mediators, bringing to bear an objective and disinterested view and with power to impose, or exert major influence upon, final judgment? Or are they defenders of traditional merit system principles against all who challenge those principles?

Can a civil service organization successfully perform in all these roles? The U.S. Civil Service Commission exemplifies both the dilemma and a stalwart effort to perform effectively in all these capacities. It continues to draft and pronounce, for management, the standards and ground rules for personnel administration. Its chairman, under one of his several hats, is the President's principal adviser on personnel policy and, paradoxically, on *political* appointments. The commission is the initiator of most new employee benefit programs and the administrator of several. It is the leader of programs to eliminate discrimination in employment against minority groups, against women, against the handicapped. It is the guide and monitor of employee relations programs and the place of final appeal from certain kinds of adverse action—a role which calls for neutrality and objectivity. Finally, it continues to be the principal guardian of the older merit principles—open and equal competition, position classification, equal pay for equal work, etc. Whether and for how long the Commission can successfully maintain this four-directional posture is questionable. Not long after the Kennedy orders, rumblings from the labor sector and collective bargaining enthusiasts began to be heard against the commission's guidelines and advice to agencies relative to their implementation.[13] In general, the charges alleged a general bias against genuinely bilateral co-operation between management and labor, restriction of the subject-matter range of collective bargaining to the minimum, neutrality rather than active support for the extension of the bargaining principle, and preservation of the unilateral ideology of the traditional merit system.

It is needless to argue or speculate upon these allegations. It seems very likely, however, that the historic posture, the statutory responsibilities, and the popular image of civil service organizations make such criticisms inevitable. As public employees organize and become more militant, they are almost bound to cast civil service organizations in the role of staff arms to management, whatever independence and impartiality may be claimed. Few at any level of government are likely to be perceived as NLRB equivalents. Labor organizations may prove a more potent force in driving public personnel administration into the arms of management than the "management movement," epitomized by the Brownlow Committee, ever was. In the words of the 1960 edition of *Municipal Personnel Administration:* "The growing activity and influence of employee unions . . . has been a major factor too in bringing the personnel agency from its tradi-

13. See, for example, Wilson R. Hart, "The Impasse in Labor Relations in the Federal Civil Service," *Industrial and Labor Relations Review,* V. 19, January 1966, pp. 175–89.

tional relatively isolated position into a closer working relationship with line management." [14] The personnel director of the City of Philadelphia recently wrote: ". . . I find it very easy to answer the question as to who the personnel director represents in management-employee relations activities. No question about it. He represents management." [15] This view was affirmed by a principal public employee union leader: "The role of the civil service commission is not regarded by the workers as that of a third, impartial party; to most of them, the commission is felt to represent the employer." [16]

The organizational question discussed above is but a reflection of a more profound dilemma: the relations between the traditional principles and practices of the merit system and those of collective bargaining. Can the two be made compatible? If public employees are to bargain equally on the conditions of their employment, does this not by definition authorize bargaining on the very principles of merit? A number of personnel officials have stoutly asserted that the two are not in essential conflict. The chairman of the U.S. Civil Service Commission wrote that: "Throughout the new [Kennedy] regulations runs the theme that the public interest must be served. And nowhere in the directives does the substance of the . . . cooperation program conflict with the merit principle." [17] A commissioner of the Wisconsin Employment Relations Board, while acknowledging that collective bargaining will have an impact on the merit system, is confident that ". . . an accommodation can be found by which the essentials of the merit system with respect to the recruiting, hiring and

14. Chicago, Internatioal City Managers' Association, 6th ed., 1960, p. 288.
15. Foster B. Roser, "Role of Staff Agencies in Employee Relations," in Kenneth O. Warner (ed.), *Developments in Public Employee Relations* (Chicago, Public Personnel Association, 1965), p. 80.
16. Jerry Wurf, International President, American Federation of State, County, and Municipal Employees, AFL-CIO, in a letter to *Public Personnel Review*, January 1966, p. 52.
17. John W. Macy, Jr., "Employee-Management Cooperation in the Federal Service," in Kenneth O. Warner (ed.), *Management Relations with Organized Public Employees* (Chicago, Public Personnel Association, 1963), p. 218.

establishment of standards for promotion and training will be preserved." [18]

Others are less sanguine. The general manager of the Los Angeles City Civil Service Department in an article provocatively titled "Shall We Bargain Away the Merit System?" listed a variety of reasons why we might.[19] And the executive secretary of the Ohio Civil Service Employees Association, who may have a special interest in the matter, has written: "The unionization of employees and the trend toward collective negotiations in the public service must result, if carried to the ultimate extreme, in the eventual abandonment of merit, or civil service systems, as we have known them. . . . To destroy merit systems, therefore, is a perfectly logical objective of unions no matter how often it is denied by organizers. . . ." [20]

Some of the issues of the actual or potential collisions between collective bargaining and traditional merit principles are illustrated below:

Subject	Collective Bargaining	Merit Principles
employee participation and rights	union shop, closed shop, or maintenance of membership	equal treatment to each employee
	exclusive recognition	open shop (if any recognition)
recruitment and selection	union membership and/or occupational license	open competitive examination
	entrance at bottom only	entrance at any level
promotion	on basis of seniority	competitive on bases of merit (often including seniority)
classification of positions	negotiable as to classification plan, subject to grievance proce-	intrinsic as to level of responsibilities and duties on basis of

18. Letter of Arvid Anderson in *Public Personnel Review*, op. cit. p. 56.
19. Muriel M. Morse, in *Developments in Public Employee Relations*, op. cit. pp. 154–61.
20. Nelson Watkins in a letter to *Public Personnel Review*, op. cit. p. 58.

Subject	Collective Bargaining	Merit Principles
pay	dure as to allocation negotiable and subject to bargaining power of union	objective analysis on basis of analytically balanced pay plan and, for some fields, subject to prevailing rates
hours, leaves, conditions of work	negotiable	on basis of public interest as determined by legislature and management
grievances	appealed with union representation to impartial arbitrators	appealed through management with recourse to civil service agency

In essence these differences may be reduced to two related issues: first, the extent to which the conditions of employment will be determined on the basis of a bilateral philosophy, which accords the employees a voice equal to that of the employing government; second, the extent to which the terms of employment will be based upon collective as distinguished from individual considerations. The first of these involves basic concessions in the historic concept of sovereignty—of the patrimonial view of the state, the paternalistic view of its employment, the concept that a public job is a privilege and not a right—to the extent that a private job is a right. The second calls for modifications in the ideal of individualism in the merit system as it developed in this country: that each person would be considered on his distinctive merits in comparison and competition with all others. The wishes of the individual in his relations with his employing institution—the government—give way to those of the group acting in concert, a more equal confrontation.

How far and how fast public employment will move in these directions are problematical. But the directions are unmistakable, and the movement seems to be gathering momentum. Yet it is far from even or universal in its relevance. Local employment is moving faster than state, the manual and blue-collar worker faster than the administrative and clerical worker. Somewhat surprisingly, among the most aggressive are certain categories of professionals, especially those principally employed by and therefore principally dependent upon public employers: school teachers, social workers, nurses and other hospital specialists. It is worth noting that the concessions now being demanded by the labor movement with respect to unilateralism and individualism are essentially parallel to those demanded by the organized professions and their career services (as described in the preceding chapters). Both constitute challenges to the traditional civil service as we have come to know it. So far, and in most places, the professions have made the greater inroads. But the development of each presents the fundamental confrontation of political and administrative generalism and of personnel specialism by collectivized, organized, occupational groupings.

* * *

What does all of this mean for democracy and the public service? A principal argument for collective bargaining, in fact, emphasizes democracy. Bargaining provides the opportunity for participation by those most concerned in determining the conditions and the rewards of their work, for maintaining human dignity in the work situation, for actualizing the self against the stultifying or infantilizing effects of authoritarian rule. In the words of Secretary of Labor Willard Wirtz: "Collective bargaining is industrial democracy." [21]

Few would challenge the Wirtz definition or argue that, in principle, public employees should be deprived of industrial democracy any more than private employees. Yes . . . but! The defenders of governmental hegemony and of civil service urge that collective bargaining, unless circumscribed by narrow boundaries, threatens political democracy, the ultimate

21. W. Willard Wirtz, *Labor and the Public Interest* (New York, Harper & Row, 1964), p. 57.

power of the citizen through his general representatives to control the destinies of government and the conditions whereby it employs its personnel.

Clearly there are dangers, but the dangers are on both sides. Those in the private sector are as great as, if not greater than, those in the public. A review of the record so far compiled suggests that political democracy has not been seriously threatened by public unionism and collective bargaining except in a few scattered instances. In a great many governmental jurisdictions the wages and conditions of work are sub-standard; in some they are disgraceful. These can hardly enhance the quality of recruitment and of service, any more than they can improve the worth and dedication of public servants. If unionization and genuine collective bargaining can improve such conditions, it is certainly in the public interest—as well as the interest of the employees—that they be encouraged.

But this calls for an enlightened policy on the part of public employee organizations. Neither the public nor the members of such organizations will be served by policies discouraging initiative, education, training, and dedication to service. The appointment and the reward systems must recognize achievement and promise, not alone union membership and seniority. The most cogent argument against some public unions today concerns not political democracy and popular sovereignty, but their pressure toward conformism and mediocrity.

Finally, it is frequently observed that public employee organizations are increasingly pressing for changes in public policy in, or related to, their particular fields of endeavor. Thus they are infringing upon the prerogatives of elective and appointive officials who are responsible to the public for policy decisions. Their influence on policy at this time is very much less than that of professional groups both inside and outside governmental employ. Nonetheless their influence is considerable, and it is growing. Most employee demands— those regarding wages, hours, working conditions—call for increased expenditures, which in turn necessitate rising budgets and taxes. These are central to policy and politics, especially at local and state levels. Increasingly these demands are augmented by demands for improved programs and operations: reductions in welfare case loads, reductions in hospital patients per nurse, reduction in pupils in the classroom, etc. Most of these demands accord with—or fall short of—approved standards set by accredited professional organizations in the various fields. This suggests that the policy aspirations of most employee organizations to this date are neither exorbitant nor unreasonable. Many indeed are minimal in relation to needs and clientele requirements.

At this stage in history, employee organization and collective bargaining offer some promise of greater personal democracy in terms of individual dignity and participation. Their threat to political democracy is scattered but on the whole seems slight. Their denial would appear contradictory to effective democracy, however defined.

7

Merit, Morality, and Democracy

OVER THE CENTURY which separated the presidencies of Andrew Jackson and Franklin D. Roosevelt, the people of the United States built an ideology which related the public service to their indigenous concepts of democracy in a unique but basically coherent fashion. The ideology came to be known as "merit principles" and the methods devised to give them effect as "merit system." *Merit* became the administrative expression and foundation of democratic government. As President Theodore Roosevelt said in his first message to Congress in 1901: "The merit system of making appointments is in its essence as democratic and American as the common school system itself." The goals, the norms, and the criteria of merit systems were unambiguous and widely agreed upon. This is attested by the repetitiveness of countless studies at all levels of government which aimed to strengthen democracy through improved personnel practices. Until World War II few such studies failed to recommend extension of civil service coverage, improved competitive examinations, precise job classifications, and "equal pay for equal work." A neutral, efficient civil service was viewed as not merely desirable; it was essential to democracy itself.

Developments in the second third of the twentieth century have befogged the meaning of merit principles and confused the content of merit systems. The reasons for this growing ambiguity are partly semantic. No doubt many Americans equate the merit system of employment with trappings and practices inherited from the past and held to be of questionable value and declining relevance today: independent civil service commissions, paper and pencil tests, individual job "ownership," unchallengeable job security, paperwork, and red tape. The real sense of "merit principles," however, is a good deal more profound than these popularized views, and the doubts about its current applicability go well beyond questions of semantics. They derive from changes in the society, its ethos, its educational system, its vocational structure —changes so extensive that one wonders whether the old "merit principles" will ever again be operational.

The merit ideology was the progeny of many different parents. Their combination of genes produced an unusual child which, as suggested above, grew into a reasonably solid, consistent, and even handsome adult. Chief among the parents was the Protestant Ethic: respect for, even worship of, work not merely as a practical necessity but as a high moral imperative. As it applies to employment, the word *merit* bears two connotations, both dominantly ethical. One is the sense of deserving and rewarding on the basis of past performance or demonstration (for example, in competitive examination). Work is fundamentally good, desirable, meritorious; the reward for the deserving is the job or the promotion. The second connotation of merit concerns the grounds or criteria of consideration and judgment. A judge considers an argument on its merits; a scientist considers a proposition on its merits; an employing officer considers a prospective or current employee on his merits. In all three usages, merits have to do with considerations of intrinsic, relevant value or truth. Negatively, the considerations scrupulously discard any irrelevancies—whether legal technicalities, or useless scientific data, or factors unrelated to one's worthiness to perform a job of work. In its early days merit system reform paid more attention to the negative aspect, the elimination of the irrelevancies, than to the positive. The primary extrinsic (irrelevant) ingredient at the beginning was political considerations; others (originally or subsequently) were race, religion, evidence of formal education, family relationship, friendship, and personality attributes.[1] Later, as job specialism developed, so did the sciences of job analysis and aptitude measurement. The positive connotation of merit assumed a more definite shape: the measured capacity to perform a specific type of work.

Beyond the Protestant Ethic there were a number of other contributors to the unusual character of American ideals of public service merit. Among these some of the principal ones were:

heavy stress on the *individual,* measured on his own "merits" in competition with everyone else;

egalitarianism—an open service with equal treatment for all (though within unstated limits) regardless of family, race, religion, social status, formal education, political affiliation;

scientism—faith that there is a correct solution to every personnel question that can be discovered objectively and scientifically: a best person for each job, a correct placement for each person, an accurate classification for each position, a correct wage for each class, and so on;

separatism—resting on the double foundation of non-political merit and scientism, personnel work removed from the rest of government and conducted disinterestedly, scientifically, and independently;

unilateralism—government as sovereign, and its decisions, when reached through proper procedures, final.

The Protestant Ethic with respect to work carries no such compelling authority in our society as it once did, particularly

---

1. But never have *all* the extrinsic elements been eliminated. Thus, status as a veteran of a foreign war, particularly a disabled veteran, or a widow of a veteran gave (and still gives) one preferment in employment and, in some places, in advancement. Likewise, at one or another time and place in our history we have offered employment preference on such non-merit grounds as sex, age, and physical handicap. Economic need was a qualifying factor for employment in some agencies of the New Deal, and, as discussed later, is currently re-emerging to challenge merit purism.

among youth and the disadvantaged. The phenomena described in the three chapters just preceding—professionalism, career systems, and collective bargaining—have all challenged it and the other parents of merit principles. Some of the elements long considered extrinsic to merit have become part of the "main course": e.g. transcripts of educational achievement, professional ascription, membership in appropriate organizations, evidences of political or programmatic sympathy with public hiring agency, political loyalty, personal "suitability." In fields of employee shortage—and these include most of the professions—there is little competition at entrance or in advancement until one reaches the upper grades. Career systems and labor organizations alike seek to protect their members from the competition of outsiders and also tend to reduce competition among their members on the basis of "merit," substituting the less controversial criterion of seniority. Much of the public service is now careerized; and this means, by and large, that large sectors of it are substantially closed rather than open services. While the scientific drive is on the ascendancy in most fields of knowledge, it seems in personnel administration to be giving ground: to the professions, to the universities, and to collective bargaining. Labor organizations are dislodging civil service commissions from their traditional—and still often cherished—posture of independence and driving them into the arms of management. The concept of unilateralism is directly challenged by both collective bargaining and professionalism, each of which demands increasing influence of employees and their organizations upon governmental decisions.

It is interesting that over many decades the development of civil service, the career systems, the professions, and organized labor had a common enemy: politics and patronage. Perhaps this is why, for the most part, they were accommodating and mutually supportive toward one another.[2] But in the

2. The same common enemy may also explain the mutually supportive attitudes over the years between the veterans' organizations and civil service.

places, and to the extent, that the common enemy has been beaten back, it has abandoned the battleground to the former allies, who must contest with each other. One thing seems clear: that the principles of merit and the practices whereby they were given substance are changing and must change a good deal more to remain viable in our society. We can of course continue to use the word, and perhaps we should. But let us not deceive ourselves as to its changing meaning in relation to: the determining of merit qualifications; the relations of these to jobs, decisions, and performance in government; the locus of control over job definition and applicant evaluation. We can still have merit systems, but they are not the same as those we inherited from the past and still teach (or delude) ourselves about.

MERIT AND THE UNDERPRIVILEGED

The ideals which gave support to merit principles were of course never fully realized. In fact, given the gross imperfections in American society and its toleration of discrimination and of a more or less permanently underprivileged minority, some of those ideals were, in part at least, mutually incompatible. The concept of equal treatment hardly squares with competitive excellence in employment when a substantial part of the population is effectively denied the opportunity and/or the motivation to compete on an equal basis through cultural and educational impoverishment. The recent awakening of the United States and some of its governments to the problems of racial minorities, of poverty, of the ghettos, presents another challenge to merit principles and one which promises to grow in the future. There is little agreement

---

Employment preference on the basis of war experience or disability or widowhood can hardly be reconciled with a "pure" definition of merit. As one student put it: "We know it (veterans' preference) as essentially the negation of merit." (John F. Miller, "Veteran Preference in the Public Service," *Problems of the American Public Service,* Commission of Inquiry on Public Service Personnel, New York, McGraw-Hill Book Company, 1935, p. 309.) But both merit and veterans opposed patronage.

about the various strategies which have been suggested to alleviate and hopefully correct the problems, nor about the vigor with which they should be pursued. But two points are quite clear. First, the nation is committed to do something; it cannot again bury its head in the sand. Second, a key element in both the short and the long range will be employment.

Among the fastest growing employers in the nation are governments, particularly at the state and local levels where the employment growth rate is running about four times higher than the national average. As federal programs develop for educating, training, and retraining the unemployed and underemployed, there is, and increasingly will be, pressure on the governments to hire substantial numbers of the poor and particularly the products of these programs. Already this pressure has been reflected in efforts to relax or otherwise modify accustomed civil service practices to accommodate this new demand. Among the changes which have been proposed —most of which have already been tried in one jurisdiction or another—are:

restructuring and redesigning work so that new, lower-level jobs with minimal qualification requirements are created to assist professional and administrative personnel (e.g. the federal MUST program: Maximum Utilization of Skills and Training);

re-examining and, as far as possible, reducing educational and experience requirements for lower level positions, and eliminating certain disqualifications, such as arrest records;

designing training programs specifically for governmental types of work; assuring trainees of appointments on completion of training, or even appointing them prior to training;

waiving competitive examinations for appointments;

systematically developing programs for training and advancement of the poor in planned, lifetime careers—the "new careers" program;

expanding or improving public services for the primary purpose of creating new jobs for the underprivileged (e.g. the proposal that the Post Office return to twice-a-day home delivery of mail).

Some of these actions may be taken without doing violence to traditional merit principles. The first one listed, for example, may contribute to over-all efficiency by alleviating the pressure for professionals in fields in which they are in short supply. But others almost dictate a departure from the traditional criterion of merit and the competitive principle with which it is associated. Insofar as they provide preference in public employment for the poor—and perhaps absolute preference—they are substituting for, or adding to, merit the criterion of need. It should be noted that this is not the first time that government employment has been used for the primary purpose of benefiting the employees. This practice was widely utilized during the New Deal period, particularly by the WPA (Works Projects Administration). But there is a significant difference. The New Deal programs were conceived and administered as temporary; they provided work for the unemployed until such time as the economy returned to its feet—as it turned out, until World War II. WPA workers acquired no tenure in their jobs. The various undertakings of the poverty program, on the other hand, are intended to provide permanent employment opportunities, hopefully with rising expectations of progressive careers. In those jurisdictions which have civil service laws, the new appointees would acquire civil service status.

It is therefore not surprising that there is growing concern among many civil service proponents that they must protect merit principles against the more radical proposals of the poverty program. On the other hand, representatives of the poor in the local councils and of the OEO organizations themselves at all levels are increasingly impatient with civil service for moving too slowly, not creating enough job and career opportunities for the poor, not providing quick, easy, and non-competitive processes for employment. Further, they can assert with some justice that the civil service claims of equal opportunity and open service never really applied to a substantial minority of the American population. Tensions between the poverty program and civil service are inevitable and will probably grow warmer in the future. How far merit principles must or will "give" in this struggle is a guess. But clearly they will have to make some accommodations at the bottom of the public employment ladder as well as in the middle.

ADMINISTRATIVE MORALITY

During this period when the traditional principles of merit are being challenged, similar forces are undermining the old articles of faith through which administration and democracy were reconciled. The ideological crutch which segregated policy and politics from administration can today hardly satisfy any but the blind or those who wilfully close their eyes. The ideal of objective responsibility is increasingly threatened by both professionalization and unionization with their narrower objectives and their foci upon the welfare and advancement of their members. At the same time, the idea of representative bureaucracy has acquired a meaning which is not altogether reassuring to the general public interest. Most of the professions are well represented in their appropriate enclaves, as are most of those growing categories of employees who join in collective organizations. Even the poor may now lay some claim to representation in the community councils, though its effectiveness is at least questionable. But who represents that majority of citizens who are not in any of these groups?

The problems introduced in the opening chapter of this study appear not to have been resolved through the developments described in the later chapters. On the contrary, they have been aggravated. The knowledge explosion and the

tremendous growth of higher education have greatly en-
hanced the technical and cognitive capacities of the public
service to perform its tasks. At the same time, may they not
have weakened its concern for, and competence in, reaching
social decisions responsibly with the full polity in view?

This is essentially a moral question; indeed it is *the* moral
question of the public service in American democracy. Among
the larger units of American government, the older and more
overt violations of individual honesty and trust have been
minimized. In terms of the billions of dollars involved in
governmental transactions every month the amount of theft,
fraud, bribery, and even expense account padding are today
comparatively trivial. Few sectors of American society are
more honest and more carefully policed in these regards than
the administrative arms of its larger governments.

The harder and infinitely more important issue of administrative morality today attends the reaching of decisions on
questions of public policy which involve competitions in
loyalty and perspective between broad goals of the polity (the
phantom public interest) and the narrower goals of a group,
bureau, clientele, or union. Chester I. Barnard defined administrative responsibility as primarily a moral question or,
more specifically, as the resolution of competing and conflict-
ing codes—legal, technical, personal, professional, and organizational—in the reaching of individual decisions.[3] Barnard
wrote primarily of business administration; students of government would add a less definable but nevertheless all-
important code—the public benefit.

The danger is that the developments in the public service
of the mid-century decades may be subtly, gradually, but profoundly moving the weight toward the partial, the corporate,
the professional perspective and away from that of the general
interest. In this connection a number of developments noted
earlier may be reviewed:

3. In *The Functions of the Executive* (Cambridge, Harvard University Press,
1948), Chapter XVII.

the tendency of "elite" professions to dominate the governance
of bureaus and other public agencies;
the dominance in matters of recruitment, selection, and advancement of professional groups, both in and outside government, and the waning influence of general government
(i.e. civil service) agencies;
the deepening of professional specializations;
the development of self-governing professional career systems
within public agencies;
the corporatism of organized public employees, especially those
in professional and sub-professional fields.

The multifarious systems of American government include
a variety of built-in institutional and procedural devices to
protect against narrowly based, functionally parochial decisions. Most familiar are the divisions and sharing of functions
and powers of government among different levels and units;
the division and sharing of powers among executive, legislative, and judicial branches; the various devices of executive
co-ordination and control, including particularly the executive budget; and appointive political leadership. Clearly,
however, occupational groups can successfully overpass most
of these hurdles, and in some cases indeed use them to their
own power advantage. The division of official and legitimate
power among many satrapies (units of government, executive
bureaus, legislative committees) strengthens the influence of
the unified occupational group which has a common perspective and objective as well as active participants at all levels
and in and outside of many units.

As Paul H. Appleby demonstrated in his lectures on *Morality and Administration in Democratic Government*,[4] the traditional and popularized protections against immorality in
public administration—checks and balances, decentralization,
federalism, and others—are a good deal less than effective. In
fact their protective value is probably, on balance, negative.
Appleby relied instead on two other (and in considerable

4. Baton Rouge, Louisiana, Louisiana State University Press, 1952.

degree antipodal) institutional mechanisms to assure morality in the public service. One is found in the workings of an
open system of politics whereby administrative behavior and
decisions must ultimately be judged against their potential
influence in the ballot box. Any effort to remove an area of
governmental activity from general political responsibility—
to "protect" it from politics is, per se, a threat to administrative morality since it encourages the administrator to approach his problems narrowly, to minimize or neglect or
ignore the general interest.

The second protective mechanism, according to Appleby,
is hierarchy within administration which, if effective, forces
important decisions to higher levels of determination or at
least higher levels of review where perspectives are necessarily
broader, less technical and expert, more political. Unlike
most other writers on administration of his time, Appleby
minimized the significance of hierarchy as a basis of authority.
He liked to quote Chester Barnard to the effect that ". . . experienced and effective administrators prefer not to use authority." [5] Hierarchy, on the other hand, is a means to
broaden the perspective for, and the responsibility of, decision.

The establishment of professional enclaves within public
agencies is of course a very direct threat to both of Appleby's
protective mechanisms: open politics and responsible hierarchy. By removing itself as far as possible from the normal
channels of political complaint, debate, and appeal, a professionally dominated agency denies the general public the opportunity for democratic direction and decision. By closing
the elite of the hierarchy to all but professionals, it denies
assurance of broadly based and disinterested judgment on
problems.

In fact, Appleby perceived as dangers to democracy many
of the developments noted in earlier chapters of this volume.
He felt, even more vigorously than some of his contemporar-

5. Ibid. p. 205.

ies, the danger of experts being "on top rather than on tap."
"Perhaps there is no single problem in public administration
of moment equal to the reconciliation of the increasing dependence upon experts with an enduring democratic reality."[6] He
feared that functional specialization within agencies would
result in "relative inattention to the large public" and
pointed particularly to one form of this: "preoccupation with
subject-matter expertise, as with economics, law, medicine,
biology, physics, etc."[7]—fields that represent all the professions. Finally, he feared the effects of what I have called career
systems of personnel administration—overreliance upon promotions from within, closing the door to outside recruitment,
overemphasis upon security and seniority, etc. Were Appleby
writing today, his alarums would no doubt be shriller because
some of the recent developments were only on the horizon at
the time when he wrote of administrative morality. Professional (as against civil service) control of personnel is now
much more evident; political appointees, the broadly based
generalists upon whom he relied so heavily and of whom he
was one, are increasingly professionalized and specialized
themselves; the knowledge explosion has much more closely
linked government professionals with their subject-matter
counterparts in the universities and has given a far stronger
scientific-expertise flavor to public administration.

In his writings about administrative morality, Paul Appleby addressed himself principally to the institutional arrangements which tended to encourage or to endanger moral
behavior. He did not dwell upon the ethical problems of individual public servants or groups thereof. In 1965, this
lacuna was eloquently corrected by Stephen K. Bailey in a
memorial essay to Appleby.[8] Bailey, building upon precepts
drawn from Appleby's writings, teachings, and actions, syn-

6. Ibid. p. 145.
7. Ibid. p. 145.
8. "Ethics and the Public Service," in Roscoe C. Martin (ed.), *Public Administration and Democracy: Essays in Honor of Paul H. Appleby* (Syracuse,
Syracuse University Press, 1965).

thesized the essentials of moral behavior in public service in
two categories: moral qualities and mental attitudes. The essential moral qualities are three: optimism, courage, and fairness tempered by charity. The words in all three cases are
inadequate to the intended meaning. Optimism is the confidence and capacity to deal with ambiguous situations con-
structively and purposively. Courage is the ability to decide
and act in the face of difficulties for which withdrawal would
be an easier response and to abide by principle even in un-
popular causes. Fairness tempered by charity is demanded by
the standards of justice and the necessity that value-laden
decisions be governed by the public interest.

The "mental attitudes" which Bailey identifies as requisites
of personal ethics in the public service are also three in number. All are cognitive in nature, based upon knowledge and
understanding and therefore learnable and teachable. They
consist of recognition of (1) the moral ambiguity of all men
and of all public policies; (2) the contextual forces which
condition moral priorities in the public service; and (3) the
paradoxes of procedures. Under the first of these, Bailey
stresses the ambivalence of most public decisions as between
personal and private interests and the public interest, and as a
corollary, the morally ambivalent effect of public policies. Seldom, if ever, can a policy be either totally right or totally
wrong. In his reference to the awareness of context, Bailey
emphasizes the shifting of value priorities, the necessity of
flexibility, and the increasing difficulty and complexity of
value-choices as one rises in the hierarchy. In his reference to
procedures, Bailey again stresses flexibility; the use of laws,
rules, and procedures to promote fairness and openness; and
their abuse to prevent action and to obscure the public
interest.

The Barnard-Appleby-Bailey construct of responsibility and
morality in public decision-making provides a sound base for
a philosophy of a public service which is both consistent with
and supportive of democracy. The construct contains certain
ingredients which, though fairly obvious, are not universally

accepted or even recognized. One is that there is a high ethical content in most significant public decisions; public problems do not succumb simply to factual analysis. A second is that the standards of ethical behavior that are applicable and sufficient to a private citizen in his private social relationships are not in themselves adequate for the public decisions of an administrator. The same limitation applies to professional codes of ethics in their applicability to decisions by professionals in the public service. The public character of governmental decisions adds complicating dimensions to moral behavior. A third is that public decision problems are seldom black or white in relation to their ethical content and consequences. This is another way of saying that they are difficult and that the "best" solution is seldom without its costs. Finally—and least understood—is the proposition that politics and administrative organization are themselves the best protectors of administrative morality, provided they are open and public.

But if we can accept the Barnard-Appleby-Bailey construct as a philosophic base, how can it be made operational among administrators? Must each one learn it for himself by successive burnings of his fingers—as, for the most part, Barnard and Appleby and Bailey must have done? Not many administrators are as perceptive and sensitive as these three, and one doubts that such an experiential process would be very effective, even in the very long range. Further, it is clear that some of the central tenets of this view of public morality run directly counter to the doctrine of a number of professions which are important sources of public administrators—probably the majority of them. Most professions are at best ambivalent, at worst downright hostile toward government in general and politics in particular. Most seek to shield themselves from politics, and this of course means that they oppose *open* politics. Most oppose the incursion of non-professionals into their professional decision-making territory. Most of those which have to do primarily with things rather than people are impatient with ambiguities, with compromise, with administrative procedure. Those professions which are sciences or which emulate or aspire to be sciences—and this includes the majority of them—emphasize values and processes consistent with the search for absolute knowledge and truth. The exigencies of public problems, imperfectly defined and demanding actions on the basis of partial and often questionable information, are seldom consonant with such values and processes. The recent thrust of many of the professions is not very promising for the development of the kind of administrative morality envisaged by Barnard, Appleby, and Bailey.

DEMOCRACY AND EDUCATION

The winds of change, however, bear other straws, straws which promise new and more meaningful definitions of "merit" and also a broader and deeper understanding of administrative responsibility. One of these straws is simply the urgency of public problems. The underdeveloped populations of the world are impatient, as are our own minorities, our own impoverished, our own urban populations. Action will not wait for the completion of data-gathering and analysis or for the negotiation of boundaries between occupational monopolies. A second straw is a product of the knowledge explosion itself, which among other things has taught the interconnection of social conditions and the obstinacy of any social problem to respond to a specific, functionally defined solution. The educators by themselves are unable to cope with the problem of education, because it goes far beyond teaching. The doctors and the health officers are confronted with the same situation in the area of health, as are the police in that of crime, the transportation engineers in transportation, the welfare workers in poverty, and all of these in racial discrimination and hostility. Each profession is learning the hard way of its own inadequacies and its underlying dependence upon the methods and understandings of other disciplines. The interdisciplinary and interprofessional approach is no longer a mere academic curio, an interesting but delettantish experiment. In today's world it is an absolute necessity, for no discipline, no profession, can handle even its own problems by itself. This lesson was learned a good many years ago by the natural sciences and the "natural" professions. It is coming later and harder in the social fields, particularly economics; but its ultimate acceptance is inevitable. The interconnection of social problems and the interdependence of disciplines in dealing with them are two sides of the same coin.

Another product of the knowledge explosion has been a growing faith of the society and particularly of its leaders in the value of research to enable us more effectively to deal with our problems. This growth too started in the natural sciences and is least questioned there. It has recently spread rapidly in the life and medical sciences. It is beginning to develop in the social sciences. It is interesting, paradoxical, and indeed tragic that government has so tremendously stimulated and supported the physical sciences while giving the back of its hand to those fields of social knowledge upon which government and the society itself most immediately depend. Who first reaches the moon, and when he does it, are not of overpowering importance. What kind of an earth he returns to is. The problems of Hunter's Point, Selma, Harlem, Lagos, Havana, and Hong Kong are not going to be solved by anti-ballistic missiles or atomic energy or space spectaculars. They are human problems that can respond only to human remedies. We are only beginning to learn how to analyze these problems and to devise means of coping with them. Social policies must be focused on values, tempered by sympathy, grounded in knowledge.

The higher officials in the public service are products of the colleges and universities, and principally their professional departments and schools. This will be increasingly, even mayhap exclusively, true in the future. These persons will have a growing influence in the determination of public policy. Ultimately the possibilities of a truly democratic public service will depend upon (1) the mobility whereby intelligent individuals from all walks of life may progress to higher education and (2) the kind of orientation and education they receive in the universities. On the first point there is evidence of progress, though there is a long way to go. On the second, in spite of centripetal, problem-oriented pressures described earlier, there remains a high and perhaps growing degree of specialization in particular fields accompanied by a declining exposure to, and interest in, broader social areas, including the context within which each specialization operates.

Merit as traditionally defined is today an anchronism for a large and important part of the public service. In the future, merit will increasingly be measured by professionals against criteria established by the professions and by the universities which spawn them. It will depend in part upon technical and cognitive qualifications in the fields of specialization. The danger is that these will be too large a part of the criteria. Truly meritorious performance in public administration will depend at least equally upon the values, the objectives, and the moral standards which the administrator brings to his decisions, and upon his ability to weigh the relevant premises judiciously in his approach to the problems at hand. His code can hardly be as simple as the Ten Commandments, the Boy Scout Code, or the code of ethics of any of the professions; his decisions usually will require some kind of interpretation of *public* and *public interest*—explicit, implicit, even unconscious.

Such decisions are difficult, complex, and soul-testing, for the qualities they demand search the depths of both mind and spirit. As Bailey wrote, "Virtue without understanding can be quite as disastrous as understanding without virtue." [9] Understanding entails a degree of knowledge, a sense of relationships among phenomena, an appreciation of both social and private values. Most of the ingredients of understanding can be learned, and many of them can be taught. They go well beyond the mastery of scientific method, of substantive knowl-

9. Ibid. p. 285.

edge, of professional technique. They go beyond the boundaries of the typical profession or the curriculum of the standard professional training course. Yet understanding in this sense must become a major ingredient of public service merit in the future. This will require a degree of modesty and even humility on the part of individual professionals (and professors) about their fields; a curiosity about, and accommodation toward, other fields of study and vocation; a sense of the society and the polity, and of the relationships between them and the field of occupational concentration.

Governmental agencies have for the most part accepted professional and academic definitions and measurements of merit as applied to specific academic and occupational fields. Most of them have, however, minimized the broader understanding discussed in the preceding paragraph as an element in appointment or advancement. The more difficult, less measurable elements of morality in public decision-making have been almost completely ignored in discussions of merit principles, although they may well be the most important criteria of all.

As in our culture in the past and in a good many other civilizations, the nature and quality of the public service depend principally upon the system of education. Almost all of our future public administrators will be college graduates, and within two or three decades a majority of them will have graduate degrees. Rising proportions of public administrators are returning to graduate schools for refresher courses, mid-career training, and higher degrees. These trends suggest that university faculties will have growing responsibility for preparing and for developing public servants both in their technical specialities and in the broader social fields with which their professions interact.

The universities offer the best hope of making the professions safe for democracy.